INTRODUCTION TO BASIC

INTRODUCTION TO BASIC

Jeffrey B. Morton

Associate Professor
Department of Mechanical and Aerospace Engineering
University of Virginia

MATRIX PUBLISHERS, INC.

BEAVERTON, OREGON • USA

10 9 8 7

Library of Congress catalog card number: 77-83748

Matrix Publishers, Inc.
11000 S.W. 11th Street
Beaverton, Oregon 97005

ISBN: 0-916460-22-3

Illustrations by Scientific Illustrators.
In-house Editor was Merl K. Miller.
Printing and Binding by Pantagraph Printing, Bloomington, Illinois

Acknowledgements

There have been many people who have contributed to this book—the hundreds of students who have used the notes on which it is based, the other instructors who have not only used and commented on the notes, but also have so generously supplied projects and exercises. While the list is too long to enumerate, I want them all to know that I am deeply grateful.

I am especially indebted to Professor John E. Scott, Jr., who provided the initial encouragement and support for this project, and who read and commented on an early version of the notes. I would also like to thank Professor Ira D. Jacobson, who reviewed the final version of this manuscript and improved it with his many comments.

Last, but certainly not least, I would like to dedicate this book to my wife Judy, who provided a great deal of help and support on this project.

Contents

Preface

This book is the outgrowth of notes used in the first-year engineering course taught at the University of Virginia. Although it is an engineering course, more than one third of the students who have taken it are not engineers, but come from the College of Arts and Sciences and the Commerce School.

The course is basically divided into two parts. The first half of the course is devoted to learning BASIC, and the second half is primarily oriented to doing several of the projects.

In undertaking this task, I tried to achieve two goals. First, the student should be able to write programs as soon as possible. Second, the book, and especially the projects, should illustrate a variety of the applications of the computer.

Since BASIC varies greatly from version to version, the student will want to have a user's manual available. I have not tried to point out all of the variations one finds among the versions of BASIC. However, the material covered here is common among most versions.

1

Introduction

In recent years, there have been dramátic changes in the nature of computers. They come in many different forms ranging from individual "kits" that you can put together yourself to highly sophisticated time-sharing systems. Time-sharing systems are, as the name implies, computers designed to allow a large number of people to use them simultaneously. The computer is so fast compared with the human thought process and response time that each user appears to have the computer's undivided attention.

A new generation of computers, the minicomputer, is beginning to have a large impact on business and science. These computers, which can cost as little as a few thousand dollars, are bringing major computer power to thousands of applications which could not afford the benefits of computerization in the past. The scientist or engineer can now afford to put the computer in the laboratory and dedicate it to running his experiments and analyzing his data. The small businessman can now use the computer to do his accounting and general business operations.

The computer is a very powerful tool for the engineer, businessman, and scientist. It can do tedious, repetitious calculations; it can simulate real processes; and it can handle and analyze large quantities of information (data). It cannot, however, replace your brain; it cannot decide what needs to be done and how to do it. In fact, the computer can only do what you tell it to do, not what you meant to tell it or thought you had told it. If there is an error in your reasoning, the computer will proceed anyway, producing wrong answers. Thus, it is important to communicate with the computer in a very precise way.

To help you communicate with the necessary precision, a special language, called BASIC, has been developed. BASIC is an easy computer language to learn because it uses English words with their common meaning. There are a very limited number of instructions in BASIC, and each instruction has a precise, unambiguous meaning. By combining these instructions in groups (called programs), you can harness the vast power of the computer to do a wide variety of problems.

Computers come in all shapes and sizes, but from the user's point of view, they all have basically three parts—a terminal (input/output device), a central processor and a mass storage unit. A minicomputer usually has one of each, while a time-sharing system will have many terminals all connected to the same central processor.

The terminals used in time-sharing systems and minicomputers are usually similar. They consist of a typewriter-like keyboard with some extra keys and either a typewriter-like printer or a video display. When the video display is used, a hard copy printer is usually available also. A typical terminal is described in detail in Appendix A.

The central processor (CPU) is the heart of the system. It consists of a high speed memory and arithmetic units for doing the required calculations. The memory is used to store the program (or for time-sharing systems—programs) which is currently being executed as well as the data being processed.

Programs can be entered into the central processor from the terminal, executed, and results displayed on the terminal or printed out on the printer. These two units are sufficient to write programs, run them and get results for some simple applications. The third unit, the mass storage unit, provides a vast increase in the capabilities of the systems. This device, generally a magnetic tape or magnetic disk (called simply a disk), is capable of storing thousands or millions of characters of information.

There are many differences between the storage or memory in the CPU and the storage on the disk. The memory in the CPU is only a temporary memory—that is, your information is stored in the CPU only while you are working on it. When you finish a session on the time-sharing system or turn off your minicomputer, the information stored in the CPU is lost. On the other hand, the information stored on the disk is retained indefinitely—until you instruct the computer to delete it from storage. Access to information on the disk, however, is much slower than access to the CPU memory.

LOGGING IN

For minicomputers, the process of getting started is generally very simple and involves little more than turning the machine on. For time-sharing systems, each person must identify himself so that the system can verify his authorization. Appendix B contains two typical examples which illustrate these processes. You should look at these examples and then learn how these processes are done on your facility.

These procedures, including procedures for saving programs on the disk for future use, vary greatly from system to system. In addition, the various versions of BASIC contain different features. In this book, we will limit ourselves to the features of BASIC which are most nearly universal. Each version of BASIC has a user's manual which describes all the variations for a given system. Once you have mastered the elements described in this book, you should have no trouble picking up the additional features which are available locally from your user's manual.

GETTING STARTED

After logging in, the computer will respond with [†]

READY

The computer is now ready to accept your instructions.

To make the computer work for you, it must be provided with a set of instructions and data on which to perform the instructions. This set of instructions and data is called a program.

SAMPLE PROGRAM

Below is an elementary program which calculates the volume of a sphere with radius R. The values of R are listed in line number 70 after the word "DATA".

[†]We will use all upper case letters to indicate what you, the user, should type and underline upper case letters for what the computer types. Expressions in parentheses indicate special keys you must depress. The ↑ indicates exponentiation. ∗ indicates multiplication and / indicates division.

```
10  REM: PROGRAM TO CALCULATE VOLUME OF SPHERE
20  PRINT "RADIUS", "VOLUME"
30  READ R
40  LET V = 4 * 3.14159 * (R ↑ 3) / 3
50  PRINT R, V
60  GO TO 30
70  DATA 1, 2, 3, 4
80  END

RUN (return)
```

To get a feel for your terminal, type this program in exactly as shown. The command RUN tells the computer that you have finished working on the program and wish to have the computer execute these instructions.

The computer will respond with (print) the answer. The results should look like this:

RADIUS	VOLUME
1	4.18879
2	33.5103
3	113.097
4	268.083

OUT OF DATA IN LINE 30

The "out of data in line 30" is an error message indicating that the computer tried to read more data than was available. Whenever the computer tries to perform an operation that cannot be done or when the computer cannot interpret something that is entered, an error message is printed.

The BASIC language has a very restricted vocabulary and a very formal structure. If in writing a program you deviate either from the vocabulary or the structure, the computer will not be able to understand what you have entered and will respond with an error message.

Getting error messages is a very normal part of writing computer programs—even the most experienced programmers get error messages occasionally.

The computer can find errors only in vocabulary or grammar, not in logic. Thus, it is important to be sure that the logic is correct since incorrect logic will produce incorrect answers. As they say in the trade "Garbage in - Garbage out!"

Let us now look at some of the general features of this sample program.

FORMAT

With minor exceptions which will be discussed later, the computer completely ignores blank spaces wherever they occur. The computer would, for example, accept the line beginning with the number 30 in the example above typed in any of the following ways:

> 30READR
> 3 0READ R
> 30 READR
> 30 RE ADR

etc.

However, it is apparent that the use of blanks in appropriate places can make the program more readable. Therefore, blanks should be used to make your statements resemble English wherever possible.

LINE NUMBERS

Note that each line in the program except the command RUN begins with a number. Since the computer acts immediately on commands, e.g. RUN, LIST, BYE, they do not have line numbers. All statements, e.g. READ, GO TO, END, must have line numbers.

When the computer gets ready to run the program, it arranges the lines so that their numbers are in ascending order. It then proceeds through the program line by line unless an instruction changes the sequence. Thus, in the above example, line 10 is executed before line 20, etc. A line number can be any whole number (integer) up to four digits. When writing a program, number the lines 10, 20, 30, etc. so there will be room between them to insert new ones. A line can be inserted between 20 and 30 simply by giving it a number between 20 and 30, such as 25. This is very convenient when you wish to correct an error in a program or change the logic.

If two or more lines have the same number, only the last one typed in is retained. So, to correct a line, just retype it in corrected form with the same line number. To eliminate a line, retype only the line number.

END

The last statement (the one with the highest line number) must be an END statement. This tells the computer that the program is complete.

LOGGING OFF

On time-sharing systems, logging off is accomplished by typing

BYE (return)

The computer will respond with some closing message such as the amount of time which was used. When this is complete, just turn off your terminal. (If connected by telephone, hang up the phone.)

LISTING PROGRAMS

After modifications have been made to a program or after the program has been retrieved from storage, you may wish to have the computer print the program in its current form. To do this type

LIST

RENUMBER

Sometimes when modifying a program, you will find that you want to insert a line between two lines which are just one number apart. For example, it is not possible to insert a line between lines 25 and 26. When this happens, it is useful to renumber the program. To do this type

RENUMBER

This command renumbers all lines, giving the first line the number 10. All subsequent lines are numbered in increments of 10. All references to line numbers (such as GO TO statements, etc.) are appropriately changed. For example, type

```
1  REM: SAMPLE PROGRAM
2  READ A, B
3  DATA 1, 2, 3, 4, 5, 6
4  PRINT "A =  "; A, "B =  "; B
5  GO TO 2
6  END

RENUMBER
LIST

10  REM: SAMPLE PROGRAM
20  READ A, B
30  DATA 1, 2, 3, 4, 5, 6
40  PRINT "A =  "; A, "B =  "; B
50  GO TO 20
60  END
```

FLOW CHARTS

It is very difficult to write long, complex computer programs without carefully organizing your thoughts. Flow charts help do this while avoiding the detailed consideration, which must go into the actual computer program. Flow charting is a very personal process and there are no hard and fast rules for constructing and using flow charts.

   In order to construct a flow chart, we need to introduce some symbols.

Terminal Box

These are used to indicate the beginning and end of the program.

Process Box

Process boxes are used to indicate necessary computations or manipulations.

Decision Box

Besides the standard arithmetic operations, computers can compare quantities to determine which logical path to follow based on this comparison. It is this "decision making" ability that makes the computer much more than a super desk calculator.

Input/Output Box

These parallelograms are used to indicate where information is inputted (read in) or outputted (printed out).

All boxes are connected by logical paths indicated by lines with arrows.

SAMPLE FLOW CHART

The use of flow charts is best explained by illustration. A simple flow chart might look like this.

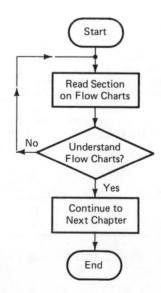

Complicated flow charts may require more than one page to draw or they may require logic paths to crisscross making the chart confusing. To eliminate these problems, it is sometimes useful to write the flow chart in sections with special symbols to indicate the interconnection of sections. The symbol usually used is a circle with a letter or a number in it.

When a logic path is broken, a connection symbol is put on both parts of the logic path at the point where they should join.

To illustrate how to use a flow chart, let's write a flow chart to show your friend (the one with much money but few brains) how to buy new speakers for his stereo.

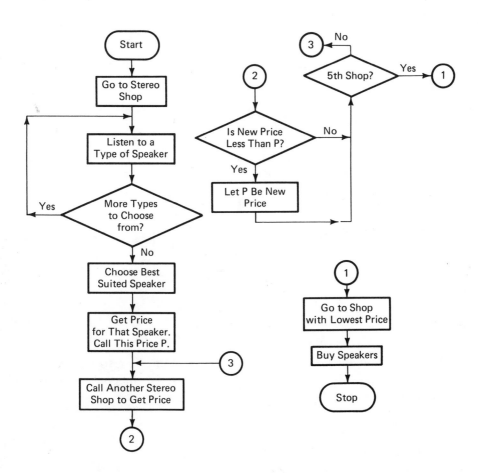

The most difficult part of writing a flow chart is identifying all the decision boxes and making sure to provide for every option. Careful analysis of the particular problem and some practice will enable you to write good flow charts.

SAMPLE FLOW CHART

We are asked to write a program to sum the squares of the odd integers between 1 and N where N is a large integer. Of course, we begin by writing a flow chart.

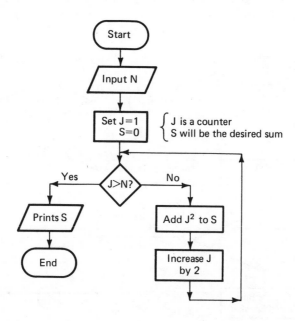

EXERCISES

1. System commands sometimes vary from computer to computer. For the computer you are going to be using, list the commands for the following operations:

   1. logging onto the computer
   2. logging off the computer

3. clearing the CPU memory

4. naming a program

5. saving a program (copying the program to a disk)

6. retrieving a program from the disk

7. eliminating a program saved on the disk

8. listing a program in the CPU memory.

2. Type into the computer the sample program on page 4 and do the following:

   a. list the program,

   b. save the program on the disk under the name SAM,

   c. run the program.

3. Write a program to print your name, address, and social security number.

4. Write a flow chart for changing a flat tire on a car.

5. Write a flow chart for balancing your checkbook.

6. Write a flow chart for calculating N!
   (Note: $N! = N * (N - 1) * (N - 2) * \ldots * 1$).

7. Play computer. Follow the steps in the flow chart on page 12 and indicate what value of I would be printed. Write all intermediate values of I, J, and K.

8. Play computer for the flow chart on page 12. Follow the indicated steps and show the value of K that is printed. Write out all intermediate values of S and K.

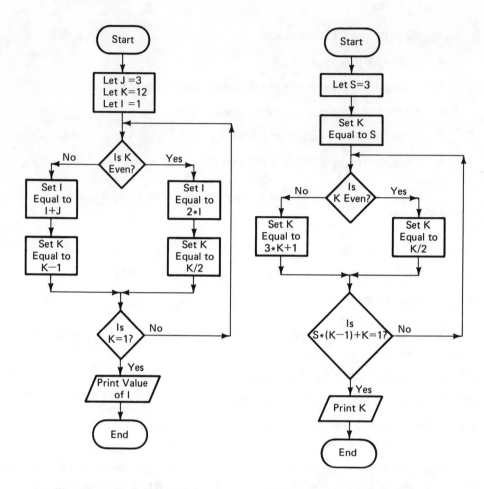

Flow chart for Problem 7   **Flow chart for Problem 8**

2

The BASIC Language

VARIABLES

Any quantity which we may wish to change within a computer program is called a variable and must be given a name. A variable name in BASIC can be any letter in the alphabet, or one letter followed by one digit. Proper variable names include:

A, B, F9, H8, T1, Z0, etc.

These variable names (there are 286 of them) really refer to locations in the computer memory. Thus when we refer to the variable A, we really mean the number stored in location A, the variable C0 (C - zero) refers to the number stored in location C0.

One way to think of variables is as storage locations in the computer. Imagine that the computer's memory is a large blackboard divided into 286 boxes. (We'll see shortly that the computer's memory is really much larger than this)

A	B	C	D
A1	B1	C1	D1
A2	B2	C2	D2

Each box is given a name, A, B, . . .

Any time we refer to the variable A in a BASIC statement, we really mean the value stored in the location A (for our blackboard example - the value written in the box labeled A).

Thus if we have the basic statement

$$10 \text{ LET A} = 3.2$$

we interpret this as put the number 3.2 in location A. Note that we can have only one number in a location at a time so this instruction also implies—if there was a value stored in A, erase it, then store the value 3.2.

The statement

$$20 \text{ LET A} = B + C$$

takes the value stored in B (but leaves it unchanged) and the value stored in C (leaving it unchanged), adds them, and stores the result in A.

Any time the variable A appears in a BASIC statement, the computer takes the value stored in location A and performs the indicated operation or stores a new value in the location.

EXPRESSIONS

An expression is any combination of variables, constants, arithmetic operations (addition, subtraction, multiplication, division and exponentiation), and parentheses.

In BASIC, special symbols are used to indicate arithmetic operations:

∗ multiplication

/ division

+ addition

− subtraction

↑ exponentiation

Expressions may be simple:

$$A$$
$$A + 5$$
$$C1 - F2$$
$$X/Y$$

or they may be quite complex

$$(((A + B) / (C1 - F2)) * E \uparrow F) \uparrow 5$$

Arithmetic operations are performed in the following order:

Exponentiation

Multiplication or Division (from left to right)

Addition or Subtraction (from left to right)

Thus,

$$A * B \uparrow C/D + E$$

is interpreted as B to the C power, multiplied by A. This product is then divided by D, and E is added to the result.

When this order of operations is not satisfactory, parentheses can be used to change it. Arithmetic operations are always performed from the innermost set of parentheses to the outermost set of parentheses.

We would interpret

$$((A + B) / (C + D)) \uparrow (E + F)$$

as the sum (A + B) divided by the sum (C + D). The result of this calculation would then be raised to the (E + F) power. When you are not sure how the computer will interpret an expression, use parentheses to ensure the correct interpretation.

Constants (i.e., numbers) may be used anywhere that a variable can be used in an expression. Constants may or may not have decimal points or signs (a minus sign is needed for negative numbers, a plus sign or no sign indicates the number is positive). They cannot contain commas. Thus 0.25 is a constant for our purposes here while 1/4 is an expression. 1/4 is a combination of two constants and one operation (/).

When evaluating an expression, the computer uses the current value of all variables, along with any constants, to produce a single number, the value of the expression. The values of the variables (i.e., the numbers stored in the location with the variable names) are unchanged by the process of evaluating an expression.

We are now ready to discuss the statements that make up the BASIC language. We shall discuss them only briefly at this time, saving until later the detailed rules and refinements.

PRINT

A PRINT statement tells the computer to type out information on the terminal.

The statement

10 PRINT A

tells the computer to take the current value of the variable A (i.e., the number stored in storage location named A) and print it on the terminal. The PRINT statement does not change the value of A in storage.

The value of any expression can be printed by putting the expression in the PRINT statement. Other examples include

10 PRINT 3 + 2   (a)

10 PRINT A + 4   (b)

10 PRINT (A + B) ↑ 2   (c)

Example (a) will result in the number 5 being typed. The value of A remains unchanged in example (b). The number that is printed out is the value of A plus 4. Example (c) will cause the values of A and B to be added, squared, and the result printed. Neither the value of A nor the value of B is affected.

More than one number can be printed on a line by separating the expressions by commas. The statement

10 PRINT A, B, 3

will cause the computer to print the value of A, the value of B, and the number 3 on the same line. Up to five items can be printed on a line using commas.

Labels can be printed by enclosing them in quotation marks. The label and the variable to be printed are separated by a semi-colon. Thus

$$10 \quad \text{PRINT} \quad \text{"SUM} = \text{"}; S$$

will instruct the computer to type the label SUM = followed by the value of the variable S. Thus if the number 6 is stored in location S, then the above statement would result in

$$\underline{\text{SUM} = 6}$$

Commas can be used to separate labels in order to print more than one to a line,

$$10 \quad \text{PRINT} \quad \text{"SUM} = \text{"}; S, \quad \text{"TOTAL} = \text{"}; T$$

Other headings and comments can be printed by enclosing them in quotation marks (").

For example

$$10 \quad \text{PRINT} \quad \text{"HELLO"}$$

would cause the computer to print

$$\underline{\text{HELLO}}$$

In addition the statement

$$10 \text{ PRINT}$$

will cause the computer to skip a line. This is useful in making the output more readable.

DATA

Almost all computer programs operate on numbers. That is, the program takes a set of numbers, called data, and performs a series of operations to produce an answer. The program is generally written so that the data can easily be changed. One way to accomplish this is with a DATA statement such as

10   DATA   6, 4, 5

The entries[†] in a DATA statement must be separated by commas. If there is more than one DATA statement in a program, the computer starts with the one having the lowest line number. It proceeds through the remaining DATA statements in order of ascending line number. It takes the data in the first DATA statement, reading from left to right and continues on to the next DATA statement, establishing a data list. For the above example the data list is

6
4
5

For two DATA statements such as

10   DATA 6, 8
20   DATA 9, 11

The data list would be

6
8
9
11

DATA statements can be put anywhere in the program.

The data list is constructed from all the DATA statements even when they don't appear together in the program. The computer, when it starts to execute a program, looks for all the DATA statements, puts them in ascending numerical order and forms the data list.

[†] The entries in a DATA statement must be constants as defined in the beginning of this chapter. Thus 0.25 may appear in a DATA statement but 1/4 may not.

READ

The READ statement is used to take numbers from the data list and put them into particular storage locations. Thus

10 READ A

takes the first number from the top of the data list and puts it into storage location A (assigns it to the variable A). The next number now becomes the top of the list. Each READ statement takes the number at the top of the data list; a number, once read is not used again.[†] More than one variable can appear in a READ statement. These variables must be separated by commas. The computer proceeds from left to right taking numbers from the data list and assigning them to the variables appearing in the READ statement. For example, when the computer comes to the statements

10 READ A, B, C
20 DATA 2.4, 6, 1.3

it takes the first number in the data list and assigns it to A, the second number to B and the third number to C. Thus, these statements set A = 2.4, B = 6, and C = 1.3.

LET

The LET Statement is another way to assign values to variables. The general form of a LET statement is

(line number) LET (variable) = (expression)

This should be read as "let (variable) be replaced by the value of the expression"

For example

10 LET A = 4

[†] The advanced programmer can instruct the computer to remake the data list so it can be used again. cf. RESTORE in your user's manual.

This statement assigns the value 4 to the variable A. Another example is

$$10 \quad LET \quad B = A + 6$$

This statement takes the value assigned to the variable A, adds 6 and assigns this number to B. The value of A is not changed as long as it appears only on the right side of the equal sign.

The equal sign must not be interpreted in the usual algebraic sense. A perfectly legal Basic statement which illustrates this is

$$10 \quad LET \quad A = A + 1$$

Clearly if the equal sign was interpreted in the usual sense, this statement would be inconsistent. But the computer has no problem with this statement. It takes the value of A, adds 1 and stores the sum in the location labeled A. Thus this statement increases the value assigned to A by 1.

A SAMPLE PROGRAM

The following BASIC program finds the value of Y corresponding to a given X in the equation $Y = A * X + B$

```
10  READ  A, B
20  READ  X
30  LET    Y = A * X + B
40  PRINT  "X =  "; X, "Y =  "; Y
50  DATA  3, 5, 4
60  END
```

The last line (highest line number) in any BASIC program must be an END statement. Typing the above program into the computer followed by a RUN command will produce the following output

X = 4   Y = 17

DONE

The DONE indicates that the computer has finished running the program.

When the program is executed, the computer sets up a data list from line 50 consisting of 3, 5 and 4. Line 10 assigns 3 to the variable A and 5 to the variable B. Line 20 assigns 4 to the variable X. Line 30 multiplies A by X, adds B (3 ∗ 4 + 5), and stores the total (17) in Y. Line 40 prints the labels for X and Y and their values.

It is important to note that a variable can be changed only by appearing in a READ statement, an INPUT statement or on the left of the equal sign in a LET statement.

GO TO (unconditional transfer statement)

The GO TO statement has the general form

(line number)   GO TO   (line number)

and is used to alter the sequence of statements.
For example,

100 GO TO 35

causes the computer to transfer to line 35 and continue from there.

One principal use of the GO TO is to instruct the computer to repeat a series of statements. In our sample program above, if we had wanted to evaluate Y for a number of values of X, we could accomplish this with the GO TO statement. That program would become

```
10  READ  A, B
20  READ  X
30  LET     Y = A ∗ X + B
40  PRINT "X =     " X, "Y =     " Y
50  GO TO 20
60  DATA  3, 5
70  DATA  1, 2, 3, 4, 5
80  END
```

Line 50 sends the computer back to line 20 to read another value of X. The computer then proceeds through lines 30 and 40. Line 50 returns the computer to line 20. This "loop" continues until the data list has been exhausted.

A RUN command would generate the following output

X = 1	Y = 8
X = 2	Y = 11
X = 3	Y = 14
X = 4	Y = 17
X = 5	Y = 20

OUT OF DATA IN LINE 20

The "OUT OF DATA IN LINE 20"[†] indicates that the computer tried to read another value of X in line 20 but found no more numbers in the data list.

INPUT STATEMENT

The INPUT statement allows you to assign values to variables while a program is being executed. This statement provides a useful alternative to the READ statement and DATA statement.

The INPUT statement is used when you wish to "interact" with the computer while it is processing your program. This interaction is especially convenient when many people are going to use the same program. Each person enters his own data, the computer runs the program using this data, but the program itself remains unchanged.

For example, the sample program in Chapter 1 which calculates the volume of a sphere, would be more useful if it were written so that the radius could be entered while the program is being processed. In fact, the INPUT statement allows us to do this. When the computer comes to a statement like

10 INPUT R

it stops running the program, prints out a question mark (?) and waits for the user to type the desired value of R and to hit the return key. When the value of R is entered, the computer starts again with the line following the INPUT statement.

More than one variable may appear in an INPUT statement. For example:

20 INPUT A, B, C1

[†] The exact message will vary from system to system.

The variables must be separated by commas. This statement will cause the computer to stop and print a question mark. The user then must type in three numbers separated by commas. The first number typed in is assigned to A, the second to B, and the last to C1.

The sample program in Chapter 1 would now look like this

```
10  REM A PROGRAM TO CALCULATE THE VOLUME OF A SPHERE
20  PRINT "INPUT RADIUS"
30  INPUT R
40  LET V=4*3.14159*(R↑3)/3
50  PRINT "VOLUME="; V
60  PRINT
70  GO TO 20
80  END
```

The RUN command would result in the following sequence:

```
RUN
INPUT RADIUS
? 1                        (You enter the 1 after the
VOLUME = 4.18879            question mark and hit the
                           return key)
INPUT RADIUS
? 2
VOLUME = 33.5103
```

The computer will continue to print INPUT RADIUS followed by a question mark on the next line until you hit the Break key immediately after the question mark.[†] The computer will respond with DONE. It is a good idea to use a PRINT statement before an INPUT statement to indicate the desired input. This makes it clear to anyone running the program what is to be entered when the question mark appears.

REM (Remarks)

The REM statement has the form

```
10  REM  ANY COMMENT
```

[†] Some versions of BASIC require other special keys to be hit to terminate an "input loop"

and can be included anywhere in the program. REM statements are completely ignored by the computer and are used to provide information for anyone reading the program. The REM statement can be used to identify the program or state the purpose of a section of the program. This sort of documentation is very important, especially when the program is used by other people. REM statements should be used to explain what the program does, how it does it and to provide directions for running it.

IF . . . THEN (conditional transfer statement)

If computers were restricted to the operations we have already discussed — the arithmetic operations, input, output, and transferring by means of GO TO statements, their usefulness would be very limited. In fact, it is not an exaggeration to state that if computers were restricted to the above operations, their impact on engineering, science and business would be very small indeed.

The real power in a computer is its ability to compare two numbers and, based on the comparison determine which of two logical paths to follow.

The general form of an IF . . . THEN statement is

(line number)   IF (comparison) THEN   (line number)

and an example is

10   IF A = B   THEN 200

In an IF . . . THEN statement, the equal sign has its algebraic meaning.

When the computer comes to this statement, it compares the value of A and the value of B. If they are equal, the computer transfers to line 200 and proceeds. If they are not equal, the computer proceeds to the next higher line number after 10 in the program.

There are six relations which can be used as the comparison in an IF . . . THEN statement. They are

A < B	A less than B
A <= B	A less than or equal to B
A = B	A equals B
A >= B	A greater than or equal to B
A > B	A greater than B
A <> B	A not equal to B

In the line

$$20 \quad \text{If } X < Y \quad \text{THEN 100}$$

If X is equal to or greater than Y, the computer goes to the next line after 20. If X is less than Y, the computer transfers to line 100.

SAMPLE PROGRAM

Going back to our earlier example, if we wanted to evaluate Y for each integer value of X between 1 and 25, we could use an IF . . . THEN statement as follows:

```
10  REM:  PROGRAM TO COMPUTE Y = A * X + B
20  REM:  FOR EACH INTEGER X BETWEEN 1 & 25
30  READ  A, B
35  DATA  3, 5
40  LET    X = 1
50  LET    Y = A * X + B
60  PRINT "X =   " X,  "Y =    " Y
70  LET    X = X + 1
80  IF X <= 25 THEN 50
90  END
```

Line 40 starts X at 1 and line 70 increases X by 1 each time the computer comes to it. As long as X is less than or equal to 25, line 80 transfers the computer back to line 50 to calculate another value of Y. When X reaches 26, the END statement is reached and the program is done.

A flow chart might make this process clearer:

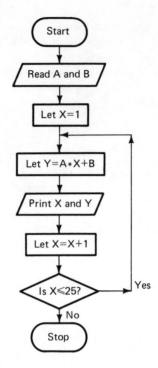

The quantities which are compared may be any legal BASIC expressions. The computer first evaluates the expressions, then compares them. For example

$$10 \quad \text{IF } (X + Y) < (A + B) \quad \text{THEN 100}$$

transfers the computer to line 100 if the sum $X + Y$ is less than the sum $A + B$.

SAMPLE PROGRAM

A quadratic equation has the form

$$ax^2 + bx + c = 0$$

where a, b, and c are known and we wish to determine x.

The solutions of this equation are well known

$$x_1 = -\frac{b}{2a} + \sqrt{\left(\frac{b}{2a}\right)^2 - \frac{c}{a}}$$

$$x_2 = -\frac{b}{2a} - \sqrt{\left(\frac{b}{2a}\right)^2 - \frac{c}{a}}$$

In order for the solutions, x_1 and x_2 to be real,

$$\left(\frac{b}{2a}\right)^2 \geqslant \frac{c}{a}$$

(Note: the computer would give an error message if you try to take the square root of a negative number.)

Below is a flow chart describing a program to solve the quadratic equation with a, b, and c entered as inputs

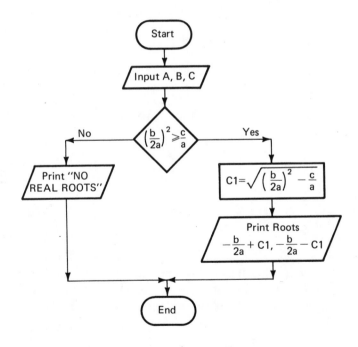

A program implementing this flow chart is

```
10  REM QUADRATIC EQUATION SOLVER
20  REM FINDS REAL ROOTS ONLY
```

```
 30   REM
 40   REM A, B, C ARE COEFFICIENTS OF A*X↑2+B*X+C=0
 50   PRINT "ENTER COEFFICIENTS"
 60   INPUT A, B, C
 70   C1=(B/(2*A) )↑2—C/A
 80   IF C1>=0 THEN 110
 90   PRINT "NO REAL ROOTS"
100   GO TO 130
110   PRINT "ROOT 1=";—B/(2*A)+C1↑0.5
120   PRINT "ROOT 2=";—B/(2*A)—C1↑0.5
130   END
```

Running this program would produce the following output

```
RUN

ENTER COEFFICIENTS
?2, 6, 4
ROOT 1=—1
ROOT 2=—2

DONE
RUN

ENTER COEFFICIENTS
?1, 0, 1
NO REAL ROOTS

DONE
```

FOR . . . NEXT

In the first sample program in the last section, we used an IF . . . THEN statement to cause the computer to do the same operations a number of times, changing only one of the variables each time. This process is called looping.

Since this process is very common in computer programs, a more convenient way to do looping is available in BASIC. This involves the use of a FOR . . . NEXT statement. The general form of a FOR . . . NEXT statement is

(line number)   FOR (simple variable) = (expression) TO (expression)
                                                STEP (expression)

(Series of Statements)

(line number)   NEXT (same simple variable as in FOR)

For example

```
30  N = 0
40  FOR X = 1 TO 25 STEP 1
50  N = N + X
70  NEXT X
80  END
```

The actions of the computer when it executes a FOR . . . NEXT loop is best explained by a flow chart

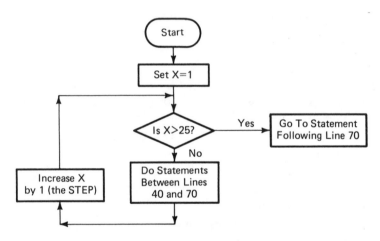

The first time the computer gets to the FOR statement (line 40) in the example, it sets the changing variable equal to the initial value. In this example, it sets $X = 1$. It then compares the changing variable with the final value (25 in the example). If the changing variable is less than the final value, the computer proceeds to execute the succeeding lines until it gets to the NEXT statement. When the NEXT statement is reached, the computer increases the changing variable by the step size and returns to the beginning of the loop. The changing variable is again compared to the final value and the computer proceeds through the loop again. This process is continued until the changing variable exceeds the final value. Then the computer transfers to the next line after the NEXT statement.

The above example used a positive step change (plus 1). In a similar manner, if the step change were negative (e.g. −2) and you had stated FOR X = 25 to 1 STEP − 2, the program would execute the lines proceeding the NEXT statement, then decrease the value of X by 2 and return to the beginning of the loop. This would continue until X became less than 1.

Our sample program can now be written as

```
10  REM: PROGRAM TO COMPUTE Y = A * X + B
20  REM: FOR EACH INTEGER X BETWEEN 1 AND 25
30  READ A, B
35  DATA 3, 5
40  FOR X = 1 TO 25 STEP 1
50  LET Y = A * X + B
60  PRINT "X =  "; X, "Y =  "; Y
70  NEXT X
80  END
```

In the FOR part of the statement, any of the expressions appearing to the right of the equal sign may be positive or negative numbers. In fact, any legal expression can be used as long as all of the variables in the expression are defined before the FOR statement.

It is good practice not to transfer into the middle of a FOR - NEXT loop. Experienced programmers avoid transferring into FOR - NEXT loops because it is very easy to make errors. Transferring out of a FOR - NEXT loop does not usually lead to difficulties.

We shall return to looping methods later and discuss them in greater detail.

SUBSCRIPTED VARIABLES

IF . . . THEN and FOR . . . NEXT statements allow us to do a series of calculations over and over again. If in the process of each calculation we compute quantities which we wish to save for further manipulation, we must give each quantity a unique name. BASIC allows us to change variable names within the program by using subscripts.

One way to think of subscripted variables is to consider them as elements in a list. For example, call the list T and call the first number in the list T(1), the second number T(2), ... , the tenth number T(10), etc.

If, for example, we wish to read in 10 numbers and put them into a list, we can use the following statements

```
10  FOR I = 1 TO 10 STEP 1
20  READ T(I)
30  NEXT I
```

If we wish to divide each number in this list by 5 all we need is

```
50  FOR J = 1 TO 10 STEP 1
60  LET T(J) = T(J)/5
70  NEXT J
```

The subscript (the number in parentheses) must be an integer since it refers to an element in a list. The name of a list is more restricted than a variable name. It may be any single letter.

The computer must be told in advance how many elements there will be in each list (for each subscripted variable). This is accomplished using a DIM (Dimension) statement. If the list T has 25 elements, then a line like

```
10  DIM T(25)
```

must be included in the program. This statement tells the computer to allocate 25 storage locations for the subscripted variable T.

EXERCISES

1. Since algebraic expressions in BASIC must be written on one line, ambiguities can arise unless parentheses are used carefully. As an example, work out the solution to the following algebraic expressions, first by hand, and then on the computer.

   a) Determine the value of X when

   $$X = 4 + 2\uparrow2 * 3/4 - 2 * 3 + 10$$

b) Determine the value of Y when

$$Y = (4 + 2\uparrow2 * 3)/4 - 2 * 3 + 10$$

c) Determine the value of Z when

$$Z = (4 + 2\uparrow 2 * 3)/((4 - 2) * 3 + 10)$$

How did your answers compare?

2. Determine, <u>without running on the computer,</u> what output would be produced by the following program and data:

```
100   READ F, G, R, S
110   PRINT F↑2, R
120   PRINT G*R, (F*G — R/S)
130   GOTO 100
140   DATA 2, —6
150   DATA 12, 4, —4, —2, 16
160   DATA —4, .5, 2.5, 1
170   END
```

After you have written your answer, check its validity by running the program on the computer.

3. Find any syntactical errors in the following BASIC statements. If the statement is illegal, write a correct statement to replace it.

a) 100   LET X = A0 + E3

b) 110   DATA, 1.5, 4, 7 + 3, 4, 5.3

c) 120   LET A= 7, B= 8

d) 130   PRINT (Q + I)/W9

e) 140   X=Y↑0.3

f) 150   LET X + 2= Y

4. The value of a dollar at the end of N years compounded annually at an interest rate of R percent per year is:

$$\text{Value} = (1 + R) \uparrow N$$

Write a program to read sets of values of R and N, producing for each set the value of a dollar at the end of that many years at that interest rate. Be sure to print N and R each time.

5. Write a program in BASIC using READ and DATA statements that computes the perimeter (4 × edge), the surface area (6 × edge^2), and the volume (edge^3) of ten cubes. The lengths of the edges of the ten cubes are 2.5, 3.5, 4.1, 5.2, 6.5, 7.4, 8, 8.6, 9.1, and 10 cm. The program should output the results in a table with appropriate headings, e.g., EDGE, PERIMETER, etc., across the top. Before running your program, test it by placing single digit values in the data statements. Then reenter the data statement with the required values.

6. Write a program in BASIC that will convert temperatures from degrees Fahrenheit to degrees Celsius or from degrees Celsius to degrees Fahrenheit. The user should be required to input a code to indicate which way to convert in addition to temperature. The program should also print instructions for the user. After each conversion, the program should ask if another conversion is to be made.

Hint:
$$°F = \frac{9}{5}°C + 32$$

$$°C = \frac{5}{9}(°F - 32)$$

7. The purpose of the following program is to determine the value of the sum of the squares of the integers between 1 and some upper limit and print the sum for the smallest value of the upper limit for which the sum exceeds 1000. The program below does not achieve this objective. Play computer, determine why it does not work properly, and fix it.

```
10  I = 1
20  S = 0
30  I = I + 1
40  S = S + I↑2
50  IF S≤1000 THEN 20
60  PRINT I, S
70  END
```

8. Write a program in BASIC that will convert variables entered in English units of measurement (feet, pounds, gallons) to their metric equivalents (meters, newtons, liters). Input first the type of quantity to be converted using the following code:

$$\text{Length } - 10$$
$$\text{Force } \quad - 20$$
$$\text{Volume } - 30$$

After the physical quantity is entered into the computer, input the magnitude of the desired English quantity to be converted. Print out the two quantities including the units. In case you forget the coding scheme, have the program print the coding instruction. After a single conversion is made, have the program ask if another conversion is desired.

Hints:
$$\text{Feet} * 0.3048 = \text{Meters}$$
$$\text{Pounds-Force} * 4.488 = \text{Newtons}$$
$$\text{Gallons} * 3.785 = \text{Liters}$$

9. Write a program in BASIC to calculate and print the sum of the cubes of the even integers that appear in the two ranges from 1 to 27, and 47 to 78 inclusive.

10. Which of the following BASIC statements are correct? For incorrect statements, write a correct statement which is as close as possible to the incorrect statement.

```
 10  PRINT "SUBTOTAL = "; C9
 20  IF J34 < 0 THEN 130
 30  FOR J7 = 1 TO 8 STEP + 0.1
 50  Z - 1 = 7
 70  IF A > B GO TO 135
 80  LET Z7 = T(0)
 90  DIM S (100), S (100)
100  INPUT R9, Z0, T1
```

11. Which of the following BASIC statements are incorrect? Why are they wrong?

```
10  LET Z + A = Y
20  PRINT A ↑ Z - 6
```

```
30  IF A = 0 GOSUB 100
40  INPUT 2Z
50  FOR I + 1 = 1 TO 8
60  PRINT "DAY=";A
70  FOR J=8 TO 1 STEP −2
80  DIM T(100), S(100)
100 LET T(10)= 3
```

12. Draw a flow chart for the following program:

```
10   REM - PROGRAM AVRGE.
20   PRINT "INPUT 3 INTEGERS BET. 5 AND 9 INCLUSIVE"
30   INPUT A, B, C
40   REM - TAKE AVERAGE OF 3 NUMBERS
50   LET Q = (A+B+C)/3
60   REM - CHECK SIZE OF AVERAGE
70   IF Q<6 THEN 110
80   IF Q>7 THEN 130
90   PRINT "AVERAGE IS BETWEEN 6 AND 7"
100  GOTO 140
110  PRINT "AVERAGE IS LESS THAN 6"
120  GOTO 140
130  PRINT "AVERAGE IS GREATER THAN 7"
140  END
```

13. Write a single BASIC statement for each of the following expressions:

$$\text{a)} \quad z = \frac{(x^2 - y^2)}{x^2 + y^2}$$

$$\text{b)} \quad z = \frac{(x^2 + x^3 + 4x)}{(y^3 - 2y)(x + 8)}$$

$$\text{c)} \quad z = \frac{x^{1/2}}{(y^{1/3} - x)}$$

3

Functions and Subroutines

Very often in writing computer programs, the same sequence of steps will be required in a number of different parts of the program. Since it is clearly undesirable to rewrite the same series of steps over and over again, we make use of the computer's ability to transfer from one part of a computer program to another. The BASIC language has two special methods for allowing us to write the sequence of steps only once, but transferring to the sequence as desired. These two methods are called functions and subroutines. Functions are used to replace simple processes. Subroutines are used for more complex ones. Both methods considerably shorten and simplify many computer programs.

There are two kinds of functions in BASIC, intrinsic functions and user-defined functions. Intrinsic functions, e.g. trigonometric functions, natural logarithm, and square root, occur so often and in so many problems that they have been made part of the BASIC language. Other simple functions can be defined by the programmer. Both user-defined and intrinsic functions are extremely easy to use.

INTRINSIC FUNCTIONS

Some of the intrinsic functions in BASIC are:

Function	Definition
SQR (X)	The Square Root of X
LOG (X)	The natural logarithm of X
EXP (X)	e^X, e = 2.7183 . . and is the base of the natural logarithm
SIN (X)	The sine of X, where X must be expressed in radians

Intrinsic functions in BASIC (continued):

Function	Definition
COS (X)	The cosine of X, X in radians
TAN (X)	The tangent of X, X in radians
ATN (X)	The arctangent of X, the angle (in radians) whose tangent is X
ABS (X)	The absolute value of X
INT (X)	The integer part of X. The largest integer less than or equal to X.
SGN (X)	The sign of X: −1 if X < 0 1 if X > 0 0 if X = 0
RND (X)	A random number between 0 and 1.

In all of these functions, X is called the argument. X can be a variable, a constant, or any legitimate BASIC expression. The computer will evaluate the expression and then compute the function. These functions can be used in any BASIC statement where an expression is used.

In the example

```
10 LET Y = LOG (A * B + C)
```

the computer will calculate A * B + C, find the natural logarithm of the result, and assign the value to Y.

Other examples:

```
20  LET Y = A * SIN (B) − C
30  LET Y = A * INT (ABS(TAN(X)))
40  FOR I = SIN (A) TO SIN (B) STEP EXP (−C)
```

The second of these examples illustrates that functions can even be used as arguments of other functions.

SAMPLE PROGRAM

A common problem in trigonometry involves the use of the law of cosines. For a triangle such as that shown below,

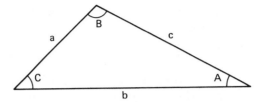

the law of cosines states that

$$c^2 = a^2 + b^2 - 2ab \cos (C)$$

a and b can be any two adjacent sides, C the included angle and c the opposite side. The following program asks you to INPUT a, b, and C. Then it prints c.

```
10  REM: LAW OF COSINES
20  PRINT "LAW OF COSINES"
30  PRINT "PLEASE INPUT LENGTHS OF SIDE 1, SIDE 2,"
35  PRINT "AND INCLUDED ANGLE (IN DEGREES)"
40  INPUT  A, B, C1
50  REM: CONVERT C1 TO RADIANS
60  LET C2 = 3.14159 * C1/180
70  LET C = SQR (A ↑ 2 + B ↑ 2 - 2 * A * B * COS (C2))
80  PRINT "LENGTH OF THIRD SIDE =    " C
90  END
```

SQR (X)

The square root of a number can be calculated either by using the SQR (X) function or by raising the number to the 1/2 power. While a complete discussion of accuracy and errors in a computer will be deferred until Chapter 6, it should be pointed out here that SQR (X) and raising to the 1/2 power are not equivalent. SQR (X) is more accurate and should be used when possible.

INT (X)

The INT (X) function is used primarily for rounding. For example

```
30  LET Z = INT (Y + .5)
```

rounds the value of Y to the nearest integer and assigns this integer to the variable Z. If Y = 3.4, the above statement would add .5 giving 3.9. The largest integer ⩽ 3.9 is 3. This is the correctly rounded value of 3.4. If Y = 3.9, the above statement would result in Z = 4.

To produce a number accurate to two decimal places, that is, rounded to the nearest 1/100, we can use a statement such as

$$30 \quad \text{LET Z} = \text{INT (Y} * 100 + .5)/100$$

The integer function operates only on the expression in parentheses so that Y is multiplied by 100, 0.5 is added to the result and the integer function operates on this. This integer is then divided by 100. For example if Y = 2.78194, we get

$$\text{INT (278.194} + .5)/100$$
$$\text{or} \quad \text{INT (278.694)/100}$$
$$\text{or} \quad 278/100 = 2.78$$
$$\text{Thus Z} = 2.78$$

If Y = 2.78691, the statement above would result in Z = 2.79.

RND (X)

This function is used to generate random numbers. Any positive number or zero may be used as the argument of RND. The results would be the same.

The statement

$$10 \quad \text{LET Y} = \text{RND (0)}$$

will produce a random number in the range 0 to 1, including 0 but not 1. Some typical values produced might be

.716283
.198437
.296538
.937135

Every time RND (0) is called, it will produce a different, random number. These numbers are uniformly distributed between 0 and 1. This means that if you divide the range into any equal intervals, e.g. 0–.25, .25–.5, .5–.75 and .75–1, and call RND (0), the number produced will have an equal chance of falling in any one of these intervals. Thus in this example, there will be a 1/4 probability that the number will fall in any particular one of these intervals.

This is very useful in simulating random processes such as flipping coins, rolling dice, or accounting for errors in an experiment.

To simulate flipping a coin, we make use of the fact that the probability of heads is 1/2 and the probability of tails is 1/2. Correspondingly, the probability of RND (0) producing a number less than 0.5 is 1/2 and the probability of RND (0) producing a number greater than or equal to 0.5 (but less than 1) is 1/2.

A program to flip a coin 10 times might look like

```
10  REM:  COIN FLIPPING PROGRAM
20  REM:  FLIP COIN 10 TIMES
30  FOR I = 1 TO 10 STEP 1
40  LET Y = RND (0)
50  REM:  IF Y < 0.5 THEN CALL HEADS
60  IF Y >= 0.5  THEN 90
70  PRINT "HEADS"
80  GO TO 100
90  PRINT "TAILS"
100  NEXT I
110  END
```

Line 30 instructs the computer to go through lines 40-90 ten times. Note that the changing variable, I, controls the number of times we go through the loop, but is not otherwise used in the loop.

Line 40 calculates the random number and assigns it to Y. Line 60 transfers the computer to line 90 to print "TAILS" if $Y \geqslant 0.5$. If $Y <$ 0.5 the computer proceeds to line 70 and prints "HEADS."

The statement

$$60 \quad \text{LET Y} = \text{INT} (6 * \text{RND} (0) + 1)$$

will produce a random integer between 1 and 6 with equal probability. Here Y could be interpreted as the result of rolling a die.

USER-DEFINED FUNCTIONS

In addition to the intrinsic functions, the programmer can define functions which are used in the same way as the intrinsic functions.

The general form of a user-defined function is

(line number)   DEF FN (single letter) (variable) = (expression)

For example

10 DEF FNA (X) = INT (X * 100 + 0.5)/100

will round X to two decimal places. After this statement, FNA (X) can be used just as if it is an intrinsic function.

The expression on the right side of the equal sign can be as complicated as necessary as long as it fits on one typed line.

Variables other than the argument may appear in the definition of a user-defined function. For example

10 DEF FNR (X) = 10 * X + Y ↑ C

Here X is the argument but the variables Y and C also appear in the expression. This statement is legitimate provided the variables Y and C are assigned values before FNR (X) is called.

The following program illustrates this point

```
10  DEF  FNR (X) = A * X + B
20  LET  A = 3
30  LET  B = 5
40  LET Y = FNR (3)
50  PRINT Y
60  END
```

In response to the command RUN, the computer would print 14.

You may use up to 26 user-defined functions, FNA, FNB, . . . , FNZ. Again, the statement DEF FN__ must appear before the function is used.

The argument appearing in parentheses immediately after the FN__ (the X in the examples above) must be a simple variable (not an expression) in the DEF statement. When the FN__ is called, however, the argument may be any legal BASIC expression.

Thus

10 DEF FNA (X + Y) = (X + Y) ↑ 2

is not allowed. However

$$10 \quad \text{DEF FNA (R)} = R \uparrow 2$$

followed later by

$$50 \quad \text{LET Z} = \text{FNA (X + Y)}$$

is allowed provided X & Y have been assigned values before line 50.

Thus, once a function has been defined, any variable or expression appearing within the parentheses (after FN__) will be acted upon exactly as the simple variable was in the definition. In the above example, (X + Y) will be raised to the power 2 and then the result will be assigned to Z.

SUBROUTINES

User-defined functions are very convenient when a particular arithmetic expression has to be evaluated a number of times in a program. They are, however, rather restricted in that the expression must appear on one line. Often in writing programs, we find that whole procedures must appear in several different places in a program. Recopying the program statements is wasteful of both the programmer's time and of computer storage. In BASIC the programmer can avoid this repetition by writing the procedure as a subroutine. Once written as a subroutine, the procedure can be included in the program at any point by using a GOSUB statement.

The general form of a GOSUB statement is

$$\text{(line number)} \quad \text{GOSUB} \quad \text{(line number)}$$

For example

$$10 \quad \text{GOSUB} \quad 1000$$

The line number after the word GOSUB refers to the first line in the subroutine. When the computer comes to a GOSUB, it transfers to the first line in the subroutine and proceeds line-by-line through the subroutine until it reaches a line of the form

$$1200 \quad \text{RETURN}$$

The statement RETURN indicates that the end of the subroutine has been reached, and the computer should return to the next line following the GOSUB statement.

GOSUB statements can appear as many times as necessary in a program. The computer keeps track of which GOSUB caused the transfer to the subroutine and after completing the work in the subroutine, returns to the next line in the program.

A GOSUB is very similar to a GO TO statement except that when the computer encounters a GO TO statement, it transfers to the indicated line without keeping track of where it came from.

SAMPLE PROGRAM

If you have N distinct objects and wish to select combinations of M of these objects, the number of possible combinations is given by $C = N!/(M!*(N - M)!)$. The following program computes C for given N and M. Note that N! is the symbol for factorial which is $N * (N - 1) * (N - 2) \ldots *1$.

```
 10  REM: COMBINATIONS PROGRAM
 20  PRINT "INPUT NUMBER OF OBJECTS"
 30  INPUT N
 40  PRINT "INPUT NUMBER OF OBJECTS TO BE SELECTED"
 50  INPUT M
 60  REM: LET M1 = N!
 70  LET N1 = N
 80  GOSUB 210
 90  LET M1 = N2
100  REM: LET M2 = M!
110  LET N1 = M
120  GOSUB 210
130  LET M2 = N2
140  REM: LET M3 = (N - M)!
150  LET N1 = N - M
160  GOSUB 210
170  LET M3 = N2
180  LET C = M1/(M2 * M3)
190  PRINT "NUMBER OF COMBINATIONS =   " C
200  STOP
210  REM: SUBROUTINE TO CALCULATE FACTORIAL
220  N2 = 1
230  FOR L = 2 TO N1 STEP 1
```

```
240  N2 = L * N2
250  NEXT L
260  RETURN
270  END
```

Care must be taken to ensure that the computer does not get to the first line of a subroutine in any way other than from a GOSUB statement. If it does, when the computer gets to the RETURN statement, it will have no place to return to and will stop executing the program. An error message will be printed out. When writing computer programs involving subroutines, it is common practice to avoid this problem by putting a STOP statement at the end of the body of the program, then the subroutines, and finally an END statement.

EXERCISES

1. The product of all integers from 1 to n is called n-factorial and written n!. For large values of n, an approximate formula for n! is

$$n! \approx \sqrt{2\pi n} \; n^n \; e^{-n}$$

    Write a program which has a user-defined function to calculate n! using this approximate formula and a subroutine which calculates n! as the product of integers between 1 and n.

    Print a table of values for n! calculated both ways for n between 1 and 20 inclusive.

2. Using the program written for problem 1, find the largest value n for which your computer can calculate n! using the subroutine (explicit method) or the user-defined function (approximate method). Note these values generally are different. (Hint: change the range of n from 1 to 20, to 1 to 1000 and note when the computer generates error messages.)

3. The purpose of the program listed below is to search efficiently through a list of numbers (assumed to be in ascending order) to find the location of a particular value. There are at least three errors in the program. One of the errors is a programming error; the others are logical errors. Play computer, find all the errors, and correct them.

```
 10  READ N
 20  FOR I = 1 TO N
 30  READ T (I)
 40  NEXT I
 50  N1 = 1
 60  N2 = N
 70  PRINT "INPUT NUMBER TO BE FOUND";
 80  INPUT M
 90  N3 = INT ((N1 +N2)/2)
100  IF M = T (N3)  THEN 170
110  IF N1<=N2−1  THEN 190
120  IF M>T(N3)  THEN 150
130  N2=N3
140  GOTO 90
150  N1=N3
160  GOTO 90
170  PRINT "NUMBER FOUND AT LOCATION"; N3
180  GOTO 50
190  PRINT "NUMBER NOT FOUND"
200  GOTO 50
210  DATA 15, 1, 1.8, 2, 3, 4, 5, 6, 6.6, 7, 8, 8.4, 8.6, 9, 10, 22
220  END
```

4. Write a subroutine to calculate the hyperbolic cotangent:

$$\text{cotanh } (x) = \cosh (x)/\sinh (x)$$

where

$$\cosh (x) \quad = (e^x + e^{-x})/2$$
$$\sinh (x) \quad = (e^x - e^{-x})/2$$

Note that sinh (x) can become zero.

5. What will be the output from the following program?

```
 5  DEF FNZ (P) = 2*P + 1
10  PRINT FNZ (2), FNZ (1), FNZ (SIN (0))
15  END
```

6. Write a program in BASIC to simulate 10 rolls of a pair of dice. The program should result in a printout of the roll number, the value of each die, and the sum of the two values printed with appropriate column headings.

7. Write a complete program in BASIC for the flow chart shown below. Use output labels and REMARK statements to make the program and results easy to read.

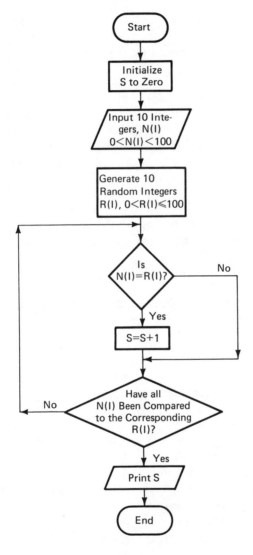

Flow chart for problem 7

8. Write a program that generates 20 integers at random in the interval -100 to $+100$ and prints out those integers (5 per line) whose

absolute value is even. If no such integers appear, the program should output a statement to that effect.

9. Given the (cubic) polynomial $y = x^3 - 2x^2 + 3x - 1$, write a program to print a table of values of x, y, the absolute value of y, and the exponential of y for the values of x between 0 and 5 in steps of 0.1. The program should print labels at the top of the table.

10. Write a drill program for multiplication which generates two random numbers between -10 and 10 and prints them out in the form of a multiplication problem and allows the user to input the answer. The program should check the answer and print an appropriate response. The program should continue to pose problems until the user indicates a desire to terminate. Upon completion the program should print the percent of correct answers.

11. Write a program in BASIC that will simulate the rolling of two four-sided dice. Randomly generate 50 rolls of the dice and keep track of the number of times doubles occur (i.e., both dice show the same number) and the number of times the sum of the spots on both dice is even. Print and label the results.

12. Write a program in BASIC to <u>match</u> the flow chart on page 49. Include fictitious values for X and Z.

13. Draw a flow chart for the BASIC program listed.

```
10   REM - PROGRAM RANGE
20   PRINT "INPUT TWO POSITIVE NUMBERS,"
30   PRINT "THE FIRST LESS THAN THE SECOND";
40   INPUT M, N
50   REM - GENERATE 2 RND. # BET. 0 AND N
60   LET X=N*RND(4)
70   LET Y=N*RND(3)
80   REM- CHECK TO SEE IF THEY ARE LARGER THAN M.
90   IF X>M  THEN 130
100  IF Y>M  THEN 140
110  PRINT "NEITHER NUMBER IS";
120  GOTO 170
130  IF Y<M  THEN 160
140  PRINT "ONE NUMBER IS";
150  GOTO 170
160  PRINT "BOTH NUMBERS ARE";
170  PRINT "LARGER THAN"; M
180  END
```

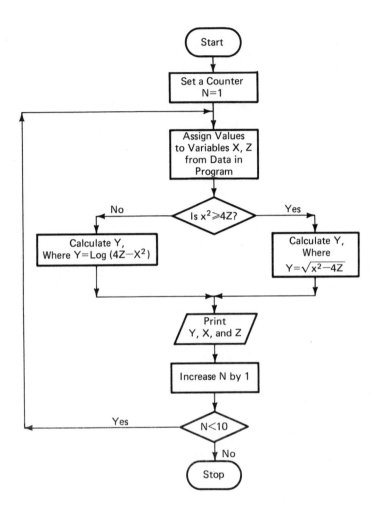

4

More on Transferring and Looping

IF . . . THEN (conditional transfer)

The IF . . . THEN statement in the BASIC language provides the ability to compare two numbers and based on that comparison, determine which logical path to follow through the program.

The IF . . . THEN statement has the general form

(line number)   IF (expression) (relation) (expression)   THEN (line number)

The relations allowed in BASIC were discussed in Chapter 2. The above statement allows us to choose between two alternative logical paths, depending on whether or not the expressions satisfy the relation.

For example

10 IF A < B THEN 100

If the current value of A is less than the current value of B, the relation is satisfied and the computer transfers to line 100. If A equals or is greater than B, the relation is not satisfied and the computer proceeds to the next line after line 10.

The IF . . . THEN statement corresponds very closely to the diamond-shaped decision boxes in our flow chart. Just as with the flow charts, care must be taken to make certain that every possible alternative is covered.

Very often, decisions are more complicated than the yes-no decision of an IF . . . THEN statement. There may be several, or indeed, many possible choices.

SAMPLE PROGRAM

For example, suppose we wish to write a program which reads in an angle and prints out the quadrant in which the angle lies.

For simplicity we shall assume that the angle (measured in radians) is less than 2π radians (360°) and is positive.

```
10   REM: PROGRAM TO DETERMINE QUADRANT
20   REM: CALL ANGLE A
30   READ A
40   LET P1 = 3.14159
50   IF A <=P1/2 THEN 140
60   IF A <=P1 THEN 120
70   IF A <=3 * P1/2 THEN 100
80   PRINT "A IN 4TH QUADRANT", "A =  "; A
90   GO TO 30
100  PRINT "A IN 3RD QUADRANT", "A =  "; A
110  GO TO 30
120  PRINT "A IN 2ND QUADRANT", "A =  "; A
130  GO TO 30
140  PRINT "A IN 1ST QUADRANT", "A =   "; A
150  GO TO 30
160  DATA 1.8, 3.7, 5.8
170  END
```

This program illustrated several important points. First, all possibilities must be accounted for. If, for example, the values of A were not restricted to the $<2\pi$ and one of the data points had been 7.2 (approximately 412°), this angle would be in the first quadrant. Note that 412° is 52° more than a full circle. Since we did not take this possibility into account, our program would indicate, incorrectly, that it is in the fourth quadrant. This happens because none of the relations in lines 50, 60, and 70 are satisfied by A = 7.2, so by default the program prints A IN 4TH QUADRANT. This program, however, works well as long as A<6.28318.

If the relations don't account for all possibilities, the computer will choose a logical path by default and it will almost always be incorrect. This is one of the easiest errors to make and one of the hardest to find.

A second point which should be noted about this program is illustrated by lines 90, 100, and 130. These GO TO statements prevent the computer from printing out incorrect information. Thus, if A is in the 4th quadrant, and statements 90, 110, and 130 were omitted, the computer would also execute the other three print statements. We must be careful to make certain that the computer does not "accidentally" exercise more than one option.

The third point to be made by this program is that care must be exercised in ordering IF . . . THEN statements. If for example lines 50 and 60 were changed to read

```
50  IF A <=P1    THEN 120
60  IF A <=P1/2 THEN 140
```

the results would be incorrect for angles A less than 1.570795 ($\pi/2$) since $A \leqslant P1/2$ also satisfies $A \leqslant P1$. Here the computer would transfer to line 120 and incorrectly indicate that A is in the 2nd quadrant.

SAMPLE PROGRAM

This program simulates the SGN function. For a given number X, it produces a $+1$ if X is positive, -1 if X is negative and 0 if X is zero.

```
 10  REM: SIGN FUNCTION
 20  REM: SIGN IS CALLED S
 30  READ X
 40  IF X > 0 THEN 80
 50  IF X < 0 THEN 100
 60  S = 0
 70  GO TO 110
 80  S = 1
 90  GO TO 110
100  S = −1
110  PRINT S
120  GO TO 30
130  DATA 6, −5, 0, 3, −2
140  END
```

Line 40 takes care of the case where X is positive and line 50 takes care of the case where X is negative. For X = 0 neither relation is satisfied so the computer proceeds to line 60 where the case X = 0 is accounted for.

FOR . . . NEXT Statements

In many applications, the same sequence of steps is repeated over and over again while changing one or more of the variables. This process, called looping, can be accomplished either with IF . . . THEN statements or with FOR . . . NEXT statements as shown by examples in Chapter 2. Each of these methods has its advantages and disadvantages which we shall discuss later. Before doing that, some further comments need to be made about the FOR . . . NEXT statements.

One of the uses of the FOR . . . NEXT statement is to sum the numbers in a list. For example, if we have a list, S, containing 100 numbers which we wish to sum, we can use the following steps:

```
100   LET S1 = 0
110   FOR I = 1 TO 100 STEP 1
120   S1 = S1 + S(I)
130   NEXT I
140   PRINT "SUM =   "; S1
```

Line 100 initializes S1 which will contain the sum of the numbers in the list. The computer goes from line 110 to line 130 for each value of I between 1 and 100 inclusive. Each time it passes line 120, the old value of S1 is added to S(I) for that I and the sum is stored again in S1. When the FOR . . . NEXT loop is finished, $S1 = S(1) + S(2) \ldots \ldots + S(100)$.

While it is good practice to write the FOR statement as shown, if the step size is 1, it may be written as

```
110   FOR I = 1 TO 100
```

The computer assumes that the step is one if none is specified.

In the above example, I is the variable which is changed each time through the loop. In many cases, more than one variable must be changed. Generally, you will want to go through the loop for all combinations of the two or more variables.

For example

```
10   FOR I = 1 TO 5 STEP 1
20   FOR J = 1 TO 5 STEP 1
30   LET Y = I ↑ J
40   PRINT I, J, Y
```

```
50  NEXT J
60  NEXT I
70  END
```

Note that this program contains two loops, an inner loop consisting of lines 20 through 50 and an outer loop consisting of lines 10 through 60. This is often called "nesting of loops."

The computer starts the program by setting $I = 1$; it then proceeds through the inner loop. That is, it sets $J = 1$, does lines 30 and 40, sets $J = 2$ at line 50 and returns to line 20. It repeats this process for $J = 2$, 3, 4, and 5. The computer then goes to line 60 where I is incremented by 1. The whole process is repeated for $I = 2$, 3, 4, and 5. Note that for each I, the computer goes through all values of J.

A flow chart for this process is shown on the next page.

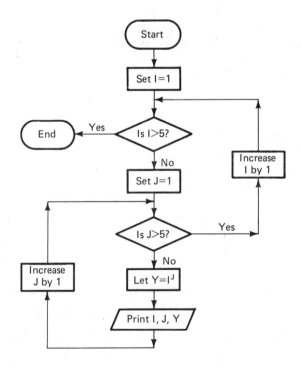

SAMPLE PROGRAM

A common problem which arises in many computer applications is to reorder a series of numbers in some special way. To illustrate how to do this, the following program reads a series of numbers into a subscripted variable S (a list S) and reorders the numbers so they are in ascending order. The original list is saved and the new (ordered) list is called T. The program also prints out both lists.

```
10  REM:  A REORDERING PROGRAM.
20  REM:  FIRST NUMBER IN DATA IS THE
30  REM:  NUMBER OF ELEMENTS IN THE LIST.
40  REM:  READ NUMBER OF ELEMENTS IN LIST
50  READ N
60  DIM S(100), T(100)
70  REM:  READ LIST
80  FOR I = 1 TO N STEP 1
90  READ S(I)
100  LET T(I) = S(I)
110  NEXT I
120  REM:  REORDER LIST T
130  FOR I = 1 TO N—1 STEP 1
140  FOR J = I + 1 TO N STEP 1
150  IF T(I)<=T(J) THEN 190
160  LET M = T(I)
170  LET T(I) = T(J)
180  LET T(J) = M
190  NEXT J
200  NEXT I
210  REM:  PRINT BOTH LISTS
220  FOR I = 1 TO N STEP 1
230  PRINT S (I), T(I)
240  NEXT I
250  DATA 6, 8, 5, 9, 3, 7, 1
260  END
```

Play computer! Take a list with, say 6 or 8 numbers, and perform each step to make sure you understand how this program works.

The purpose of lines 160, 170, and 180 is to interchange T(I) and T(J) for specific values of I and J. The variable M is used to store the value of T(I) before assigning the value of T(J) to T(I). We must do this because line 170 replaces the value of T(I) with T(J).

Clearly, we cannot replace the above three lines in our program with

```
160  LET T(I) = T(J)
170  LET T(J) = T(I)
```

These steps would make both values the same rather than inter-changing them.

If a FOR . . . statement appears inside a loop (as the FOR J . . . appears inside the I loop), the corresponding NEXT statement must also be inside the loop. Thus, a nested arrangement such as

```
┌─10  FOR I = . . .
│┌─20  FOR J = . . .
││        .
││        .
││        .
│└─60  NEXT J
└──70  NEXT I
```

is allowed, but crossing loops such as

```
┌─10  FOR I = . . .
│┌─20  FOR J = . . .
││        .
││        .
││        .
├──60  NEXT I
└──70  NEXT J
```

are not allowed.

Comparison of FOR . . . NEXT and IF . . . THEN LOOPS

The FOR . . . NEXT loop should be used whenever possible since it is much easier to interpret. All of the information about which variable is changing, over what limits it is changing, and step size are all clearly displayed in the FOR statement. The end of the loop is identified by the NEXT statement.

There is one important case where IF . . . THEN loops should be used. In a FOR . . . NEXT loop, you must know (or be able to com-pute) the limits (the beginning value and final value) and step size for the changing variable. In some problems this is not possible, e.g. the decision to exit the loop may be based on some condition being satis-fied. For these cases, IF . . . THEN loops are necessary.

For example, if you wish to write a program which flips a coin 100 times then you should use a FOR . . . NEXT loop. On the other hand, if the program is to flip the coin until 100 "heads" are produced, you should use an IF . . . THEN loop. The IF . . . THEN loop should be used since you do not know, in advance, how many times the coin must be flipped to get 100 "heads".

SAMPLE PROGRAM

We saw in examples in Chapter 3 that we could simulate the roll of a die or the flip of a coin using the RND (0) function. Simulation of random processes like these is a very important use of the computer.

There are many problems in engineering, involving both random processes and non-random or deterministic processes, which are so complicated and difficult to solve that simulation on the computer is the only practical approach.

Simulation is a technique for imitating real processes. It is useful to think of simulation as a way to perform experiments on a computer. Very often, computer experiments are the only practical ways to see how altering various parameters changes the results in a problem. For example, if you are designing a new airport, you would want to simulate the air traffic flow. You might wish to vary the arrangement of runways. Clearly, no one ever is going to perform the real life experiment of building an airport and trying several different runway arrangements.

To design a simulation, we must first develop a mathematical model for the problem. In the simulation of the roll of a die, the mathematical model consisted of the probability that a number would be rolled. For a "fair" die, the probabilities of the number of spots on top being 1, 2, . . . , 6 are all equal, each being 1/6. We could simulate a "loaded" die by making these probabilities slightly different.

For deterministic simulations, the mathematical model usually involves basic laws of physics. For example, Newton's laws of motion are used when the motion of an object is being simulated.

To illustrate the use of deterministic simulations, consider the flight of a large rocket. Newton's laws of motion are easy to formulate for this problem. However, the solution of Newton's laws is much more difficult and, therefore, we will simulate the flight of the rocket.

The form of Newton's laws which we wish to apply says that

$$F = M * A$$

where

M = mass of rocket
A = acceleration of the rocket
F = force on the rocket

We can solve this for the acceleration

$$A = F/M$$

The force on the rocket is due to the burning of the fuel. We shall assume that as long as the rocket has fuel, the force due to burning, or thrust, is constant.

The mass of the rocket is made up of two parts, the payload and shell of the rocket, called M1, and the mass of the fuel called M2. Thus the total mass is

$$M = M1 + M2$$

As the fuel is burned to produce the thrust, the mass of fuel (and hence the total mass of the rocket) is diminished at a constant rate P. When all the propellant has been consumed, the thrust goes to zero and the rocket moves along a "ballistic trajectory" until it returns to earth.

To keep this simulation from becoming too complicated, we shall assume that the earth is flat and gravity does not change with height above the earth. We shall also neglect the drag on the rocket due to the air around it. (All of these effects could have easily been added to the simulation.)

We shall follow the rocket from when it leaves the launch pad until it hits the earth. The guidance system in the rocket will make it fly straight up for T1 seconds (T1 is predetermined), then turn the rocket so that the thrust always points at an angle of R degrees from the vertical until all the propellant is used.

At any time, the vertical acceleration will be given by

$$A1 = (F * COS (R) - M * G)/M$$

G = acceleration due to gravity

F = thrust (which is set to zero when all the propellant is gone)

R = 0 until T1 seconds after launch, then has some value until all the fuel is expended.

We shall divide the time of flight into small intervals, I, or time steps and we shall assume that the acceleration of the rocket is constant within each interval.

Thus the vertical velocity changes in the interval by A1 ∗ I. The velocity at the beginning of the Nth interval is equal to the velocity at the (N−1)th interval[†] plus A1 ∗ I.

$$V1 \Leftarrow V1 + A1 * I$$

We will use the same symbol for the velocity at the beginning of the (N − 1) interval as for the velocity at the beginning of the Nth interval since at any point in the simulation, we will be interested only in the current velocity.

For the purpose of calculating height above the ground, we shall assume V1 is constant within each interval (the value at the beginning of the interval is chosen).

Thus

$$Y \Leftarrow Y + V1 * I$$

The same sort of analysis applies to the horizontal acceleration, velocity, and position

$$A2 = F * SIN (R)/M$$
$$V2 \Leftarrow V2 + A2 * I$$
$$X \Leftarrow X + V2 * I$$

For the problem, we will consider

$$F = 5,000,000 \text{ LBF}$$
$$M1 = 20,000 \text{ LBM}$$
$$M2 = 80,000 \text{ LBM}$$
$$P = 800 \text{ LBM/sec.}$$
$$G = 32 \text{ FT/Sec/Sec.}$$
$$R = 20°$$
$$T1 = 10 \text{ sec.}$$

The following flow chart indicates how we will write the program:

[†] We shall use the symbol ⇐ to mean "is replaced by."

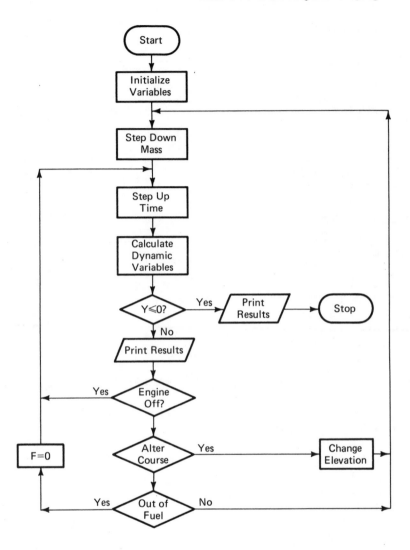

The Program would look like this.

```
10   REM: PRINT TITLE
20   PRINT "ROCKET SIMULATION PROGRAM"
30   PRINT
40   REM: INITIALIZE VARIABLES
50   LET A1 = 0
```

```
 60   LET A2 = 0
 70   LET V1 = 0
 80   LET V2 = 0
 90   LET X = 0
100   LET Y = 0
110   LET R = 0
120   LET T = 0
130   LET T3 = 0
140   LET C1 = 0
150   LET M1 = 20000
160   LET M2 = 80000
170   LET M = M1 + M2
180   LET G = 32
190   LET P = 800
200   LET F = 5.E + 06
210   LET T1 = 10
220   LET I = 1
230   REM: CALCULATE TIME TO BURNOUT, T2
240   LET T2 = M2/P
250   REM: PRINT COLUMN HEADINGS
260   PRINT
270   PRINT
280   PRINT "TIME", "X(IN MILES)", "Y(IN MILES)",
      "V1(FT/SEC)", "V2(FT/SEC)"
290   PRINT
300   REM: STEP DOWN MASS
310   LET M = M − P * I
320   REM: STEP UP TIME T, STEP UP PRINT COUNTER T3
330   LET T = T + I
340   LET T3 = T3 + I
350   REM: SAVE OLD VALUE OF VELOCITY (V3)
360   LET V3 = V1
370   REM: CALCULATE DYNAMIC VARIABLES
380   LET A1 = (F*COS(R) − M * G)/M
390   LET V1 = V1 + A1 * I
400   LET Y = Y + V1 * I
410   LET A2 = F*SIN(R)/M
420   LET V2 = V2 + A2 * I
430   LET X = X + X + V2 * I
440   REM: CHECK FOR MAXIMUM HEIGHT, Y1 (SIGN CHANGE IN V1)
450   IF (V3*V1) >= 0 THEN 480
460   LET Y1 = Y
```

```
470  REM:  CHECK FOR IMPACT
480  IF Y <= 0 THEN 670
490  REM:  PRINT RESULTS EVERY 10 SECONDS
500  IF (T3 — 10) < 0 THEN 550
510  PRINT T, X/5280, Y/5280, V1, V2
520  REM:  RESET PRINT COUNTER
530  LET T3 = 0
540  REM:  CHECK FOR BURNOUT
550  IF C1 = 1 THEN 330
560  IF T < T2 THEN 630
570  LET F = 0
580  REM:  SAVE ACCELERATIONS AT BURNOUT
590  LET A3 = A1
600  LET A4 = A2
610  LET C1 = 1
620  REM:  CHECK FOR COURSE CORRECTION
630  IF T < T1 THEN 310
640  LET R = 20 * 3.14159/180
650  REM:  NOTE R CHANGED TO RADIANS
660  GO TO 310
670  PRINT
680  PRINT "IMPACT AT T(SEC) =  "; T, "X (FEET) =  "; X
690  PRINT "MAXIMUM HEIGHT IN FEET WAS =  "; Y1
700  PRINT "ACCELERATIONS IN FEET/SEC/SEC"
710  PRINT "VERTICAL ACCELERATION AT BURNOUT =  "; A3
720  PRINT "HORIZONTAL ACCELERATION AT BURNOUT =  "; A4
730  END
```

Since this rocket flies for approximately 527 seconds, we do not want to print out T, X, Y, V1 and V2 at each 1 second interval. Since each second would require one typed line, we would get 527 lines printed out. This would take a very long time (cf. Chapter 6). To reduce the output to a manageable amount, we introduced the print counter, T3. Its only purpose is to "count" 10 second intervals to control the printing. Note that at line 500, T3 is reset to zero after printing the results at the end of each 10 second interval.

The variable C1 is used as a device to prevent the computer from going to lines 540-580 more than once. We first set C1 = 0, then set C1 = 1 at line 580. The test at line 520 prevents the computer from returning to these lines.

The command RUN would produce output like the following:

ROCKET SIMULATION PROGRAM

TIME	X(IN MILES)	X(IN MILES)	V1(FT/SEC)	V2(FT/SEC)
10	0	.204941	203.315	0
20	.200702	.808098	420.039	195.351
30	.791282	1.87638	690.79	410.367
40	1.81336	3.52414	1027.68	640.454
50	3.31855	5.89315	1447.4	978.69
60	5.37248	9.16381	1973.89	1226.79
70	8.06189	13.5735	2643.27	1686.89
80	11.5847	19.4488	3513.77	2020.2
90	15.876	27.268	4688.56	2564.87
100	21.4556	37.8011	6378.63	3295.87
110	27.6977	49.5485	6058.63	3295.87
120	33.9399	60.6898	5738.63	3295.87
130	40.1821	71.2251	5418.63	3295.87
140	46.4243	81.1543	5098.63	3295.87
150	52.6665	90.4773	4778.63	3295.87
160	58.9087	99.1946	4458.63	3295.87
170	65.1509	107.306	4138.63	3295.87
180	71.3931	114.811	3818.63	3295.87
190	77.6352	121.709	3498.63	3295.87
200	83.8774	128.002	3178.73	3295.87
210	90.1196	133.689	3858.63	3295.87
220	96.3618	138.77	2538.63	3295.87
230	102.604	143.245	2218.63	3295.87
240	108.846	147.113	1898.63	3295.87
250	115.088	150.376	1578.63	3295.87
260	121.331	153.032	1258.63	3295.87
270	127.573	155.083	938.632	3295.87
280	133.815	156.527	618.632	3295.87
290	140.057	157.365	298.632	3295.87
300	146.299	157.598	−21.3682	3295.87
310	152.541	157.224	−341.368	3295.87
320	158.784	156.244	−661.368	3295.87
330	165.026	154.658	−981.368	3295.87
340	171.268	152.466	−1301.37	3295.87
350	177.51	149.668	−1621.37	3295.87
360	183.752	146.264	−1941.37	3295.87
370	189.995	142.254	−2261.37	3295.87
380	196.237	137.637	−2581.37	3295.87
390	202.479	132.415	−2901.37	3295.87
400	208.721	126.587	−3221.37	3295.87

ROCKET SIMULATION PROGRAM (*Continued*)

TIME	X(IN MILES)	X(IN MILES)	V1(FT/SEC)	V2(FT/SEC)
410	214.963	120.152	−3541.37	3295.87
420	221.205	113.112	−3861.37	3295.87
430	227.447	105.465	−4181.37	3295.87
440	233.689	97.2126	−4501.37	3295.87
450	239.931	88.3539	−4821.37	3295.87
460	246.172	78.8892	−5141.37	3295.87
470	252.414	68.8184	−5461.37	3295.87
480	258.656	58.1415	−5781.37	3295.87
490	264.898	46.8586	−6101.37	3295.87
500	271.14	34.9697	−6421.37	3295.87
510	277.382	22.4746	−6741.37	3295.87
520	283.624	9.37356	−7061.37	3295.87

IMPACT AT T(SEC) = 527   X(FEET) = 1.52061E + 06
MAXIMUM HEIGHT IN FEET WAS = 832115.
ACCELERATIONS IN FEET/SEC/SEC
VERTICAL ACCELERATION AT BURNOUT = 202.925
HORIZONTAL ACCELERATION AT BURNOUT = 85.505
DONE

Whenever you run a computer program, the results should be checked for reasonableness. In this case, we are simulating the flight of a rather large rocket, so the fact that it reached a height of 157 miles is quite reasonable. Note that the vertical velocity changed signs at approximately 290 seconds into the flight indicating that the rocket was starting down. Also, after T = 100 seconds (burnout), the horizontal velocity is not changing. Since, intuitively we would expect it to change, we must ask why. The answer is that we neglected to account for drag on the rocket so there was nothing to slow it down in the horizontal direction.

EXERCISES

1. Write a program which generates a random number between 0 and 1000. Continue generating these random numbers until two numbers in succession are greater than 900. (Which is more appropriate, an IF . . . THEN loop or a FOR . . . NEXT loop?)

2. Write a program which generates 100 integers randomly between 1 and 10 inclusive, sorts them from smallest to largest, prints the integers after sorting in five evenly spaced columns.

3. Write a program which generates a list of 100 random integers between 1 and 100 inclusive. The program should find the largest number, print it and its locations. (Note the largest number may repeat several times.)

4. Write a program in BASIC that will compute and print a table of values of the volume of a circular cylinder for all possible integer values of the radius, R, and height H, where $1 \leqslant H \leqslant 10$. (Note that the volume of a circular cylinder is given by $V = \pi R^2 H$.) The values of the volume, V, should be rounded to the closest integer before printing, and the program should print appropriate labels for the table.

5. Write a program that will read two lists of numbers, A and B, each having 15 elements, and that will print out only the items in list B which are greater than the corresponding items in list A.

6. There are four temperature scales in common use today. They are Fahrenheit, Celsius, Rankine, and Kelvin. The relationships between them are given by:

$$°C = (5/9)(°F - 32)$$
$$°F = (9/5)°C + 32$$
$$°K = °C + 273$$
$$°R = °F + 460$$

Write a program that, when given a temperature and the scale upon which it is measured, will convert to the other three temperature scales. The program is to print all four temperatures with an appropriate heading. Operation is to be such that when given a temperature range and step size the conversion is done and execution stops. The program is also to be able to convert a list of specific temperatures and stop when finished.

The input is to be arranged such that if data are present in DATA statements, the program proceeds to do the calculation. If data are not present, the program is to inquire as to whether the user wants instructions. This will allow someone other than the writer of the program to use it and is a common situation in real-life programming.

After the instructions are given a choice is to be offered to the user as to whether the data are to be in DATA statements or in INPUT statements. If the user chooses INPUT statements, proceed at once to ask for data. If DATA statements are chosen, STOP so the data can be typed. If instructions are refused, proceed at once to ask for input data.

7. Consider a "Mexican Jumping Bean" which is placed initially at the center of an 11 by 11 grid. Assume that the bean is equally likely to jump one step up or down or left or right, and that it makes one jump every second. Write a complete program in BASIC that simulates this "random walk" process and computes and prints the time (in seconds) required for the bean to reach a boundary of the grid.

8. There are 40 students currently enrolled in ENGR 709. The instructor has decided to give only two Fs in the course, and these are to be awarded to the students with the two lowest averages. Write a complete program in BASIC that will read the final averages of the class from data and will print the two lowest averages.

5

Printing

In Chapter 2, we presented some simple input and output statements which have enabled us to get data into the program and print out the results. We saw that we could print out labels and headings as well as numbers. In this chapter we shall discuss input-output in more detail.

NUMERICAL VARIABLES

The Comma in a PRINT Statement

In Chapter 2, we pointed out that up to five variables can be printed in a single PRINT statement by separating the variables with commas. In this section, we will present a few more details about printing using commas.

The typical terminal output page is comprised of 72 columns divided into 5 major print zones. To be consistent with the notation we shall need later, we number these columns 0 through 71. The major print zones start in columns 0, 15, 30, 45, and 60. The first four are 15 columns wide, and the last is 12 columns. The comma in a PRINT statement simply tells the computer to move to the beginning of the next major print zone. For example, the statement

```
10  PRINT A, B, C, D, E
```

would print the value of A starting in column 0, the value of B starting in column 15, the value of C starting in column 30, the value of D starting in column 45, and E in column 60.

If more than 5 variables appear in a PRINT statement separated by commas, the sixth variable is printed in the first major print zone on the next line. For successive variables, the comma causes the computer to shift to the beginning of the next major print zone.

The statement

10 PRINT 1, 2, 3, 4, 5, 6, 7, 8, 9, 10, 11, 12

would result in output that looks like

1	2	3	4	5
6	7	8	9	10
11	12			

Normally, after printing the last variable in a PRINT statement, the computer generates a linefeed and a carriage return. If we put a comma after the last variable (sometimes called a "dangling comma"), the carriage shifts to the beginning of the next major print zone to wait for the next PRINT statement.

Thus,

```
10  FOR I = 1 TO 10 STEP 1
20  PRINT I ↑ 2,
30  NEXT I
40  END
```

will result in output like

1	4	9	16	25
36	49	64	81	100

The Semi-colon in a PRINT Statement

Occasionally, it is desirable to put more than five items on a line. When this is necessary, the semi-colon can be used instead of the comma. The rules for using a semi-colon are somewhat more complicated than for the comma since they depend on the size of the numeric field. Each major print zone (except the last) is divided into five minor print zones, three columns wide. The semi-colon in a print statement instructs the computer to move to the beginning of the closest minor print zone that provides at least three spaces between printed output.

For example

```
10  LET A = 5
20  LET B = 16
30  PRINT A; B; A; B; A; B; A; B; A
```

results in

   5   16   5   16   5   16   5   16   5

The semi-colon should be avoided when trying to print the output in columns, since different field sizes are used, depending on the size of the number to be printed.

For example,

```
10  FOR I = −5 TO 30 STEP 1
20  PRINT 3 ↑ I;
30  NEXT I
40  END
```

will produce the following output

```
4.11523E−03   1.23457E−02   .037037   .111111   .333333   1
3   9   27   81   243   729   2187   6561   19683   59049.
177147.   531441.   1.59432E 06   4.78298E 06   1.43489E 07
4.30467E 07   1.29140E 08   3.87420E 08   1.16226E 09   3.48678E 09
1.04604E 10   3.12811E 10   9.41432E 10   2.82430E 11   8.47289E 11
2.54187E 12   7.62560E 12   2.28768E 13   6.86304E 13   2.05891E 14
DONE
```

However, if line 20 had ended with a comma, the results would have been printed out in 5 columns.

Format for Printing

The computer prints out numbers in different formats depending on the size of the number. All numbers start at the beginning of a print zone. Numbers are printed in one of two formats; either as ordinary numbers "fixed point," such as

$$127$$
$$387.2$$
$$-127.54$$

or in scientific notation like

$$1.2E+07$$
$$-1.5E-08$$

The E+07 means $\times \ 10^7$ and the E—08 means $\times \ 10^{-8}$. This notation is often referred to as "floating point." The computer chooses the format depending on the size of the number and the number of significant places.

STRINGS

A string is a set of characters enclosed in quotation marks. Some examples are:

"HELLO"
"$/#"
"H12G"

Any character except the backspace and quotation marks may be used in a string. In Chapter 2, we saw that headings and labels, which are examples of strings, could be printed by including them in a PRINT statement.

Use of the Comma in Printing Strings

Several strings can be printed by means of the same PRINT statement. The rules for printing strings, separated by commas, are the same as for numeric variables, viz., the comma simply tells the computer to shift to the beginning of the next major print zone, e.g.

10 PRINT "THIS IS A LONG COMMENT", "ANYTHING"

results in

<u>THIS IS A LONG COMMENT</u>   <u>ANYTHING</u>

The first string in this statement is more than 15 characters so that when the computer finishes printing it, the carriage is in the middle of the second major print zone. The comma then instructs the computer to shift to the beginning of the third major print zone where it prints the second string.

Strings and variables can be printed together using the same print statement as illustrated in the following example.

10   PRINT A, "   ", B

Here the value of A is printed in the first major print zone. The string "   ", called the blank string, is used to skip the second major print zone. The value of B is printed in the third major print zone. This illustrates a useful way to skip a major print zone. Note that we cannot just use two commas to accomplish this - we must use the blank string.

Use of the Semi-colon in Printing Strings

The effect of a semi-colon appearing after a string in PRINT statements is different from the effect of a semi-colon after a variable. When a semi-colon appears after a string, the carriage is not shifted. If the semi-colon appears after a string at the end of the PRINT statement (dangling semi-colon), the carriage return and linefeed are also suppressed, e.g.

5   LET D = 7
10   PRINT "TODAY IS JANUARY"; D

will result in the computer printing

<u>TODAY IS JANUARY 7</u>

and

10   PRINT "UNIVERSITY O";
20   PRINT "F VIRGINIA"

will produce

UNIVERSITY OF VIRGINIA

Finally,

```
10  FOR I = 1 TO 72
20  PRINT "-";
30  NEXT I
40  PRINT
```

will result in a line of dashes across the page

The PRINT statement in line 40 provides the linefeed and carriage return after printing the final dash.

Commas, semi-colons, strings, and variables can be mixed in the same PRINT statement. The effect of the semi-colon depends on what precedes it. If the semi-colon follows a variable, the carriage shifts to the beginning of the nearest next minor print zone, providing at least 3 spaces between printed output. If the semi-colon follows a string, no spaces are skipped. Thus, if A=6 and B=9, then

```
10  PRINT "A="; A, "B="; B
```

results in

A=6   B=9

The semi-colon can be particularly useful in a PRINT statement followed by an INPUT statement.

For example

```
10  PRINT "A=";
20  INPUT A
```

will result in

A=?

In this case, you would type the value of A immediately after the question mark and hit the return key.

SPECIAL PRINTING FUNCTION

There are three useful functions which can be used in conjunction with PRINT statements. These are the TAB, SPACE, and LINE functions. TAB (N) moves the carriage to column N where N is a column number (between 0 and 71). If column N is to the left of the present carriage location, no action is taken. If N is greater than 71, the carriage moves to the beginning of the next line.

SPA(N) causes the computer to skip N spaces. If there are less than N spaces left on the line, the computer goes to the beginning of the next line.

LIN(N) generates a carriage return and N linefeeds. If N is negative, no carriage return is generated. If N=0 only a carriage return is generated.

For example,

```
10  PRINT "A"; TAB (10); "B"; SPA(5); "C"; LIN(2); "D"
```

will produce

<u>A</u>   <u>B</u>   <u>C</u>

<u>D</u>

Either a semi-colon or a comma may be used after SPA or TAB. In either case, the carriage is not shifted before printing the next variable. The argument of these print functions can be any legal BASIC expression. For example, if J has been assigned a value, TAB (6∗J+3) is allowed. The expression is evaluated and rounded to the nearest integer.

A Sample Program

The following program illustrates the use of the special printing functions.

```
10    PRINT TAB(8); "A SHORT TABLE OF TRIGONOMETRIC";
20    PRINT "FUNCTIONS"; LIN(2)
30    PRINT TAB (22); "BY JOHN DOE"; LIN(3)
40    PRINT "ANGLE", SPA(2); "SIN", SPA(2); "COS", SPA(2); "TAN"
70    FOR I = 1 TO 54 STEP 1
```

```
80    PRINT "-";
90    NEXT I
95    PRINT
100   REM:  FNA ROUNDS NUMBERS TO 6 DECIMAL PLACES
110   DEF FNA (X)=INT(1.E+06*X+.5)/1.E+06
120   FOR X=0 TO 90 STEP 5
125   LET Y=3.14159*X/180
130   PRINT X,FNA(SIN(Y)),FNA(COS(Y)),FNA(TAN(Y))
140   NEXT X
150   PRINT LIN(5)
160   END
```

The purpose of rounding to 6 decimal places is to ensure that all the numbers will be printed out in the same format.

The RUN command would produce the following table:

A SHORT TABLE OF TRIGONOMETRIC FUNCTIONS

BY JOHN DOE

ANGLE	SIN	COS	TAN
0	0	1	0
5	.087156	.996195	.087489
10	.173648	.984808	.176327
15	.258819	.965926	.267949
20	.34202	.939693	.36397
25	.422613	.906308	.466307
30	.5	.866026	.57735
35	.573576	.819152	.700207
40	.642787	.766045	.839099
45	.707107	.707107	.999999
50	.766044	.642788	1.19175
55	.819152	.573577	1.42815
60	.866025	.5	1.73205
65	.906307	.422619	2.1445
70	.939692	.342021	.2.74747
75	.965926	.25882	3.73204
80	.984808	.173649	5.67124
85	.996195	.087157	11.4299
90	1	.000001	890059.

Note that in the last line in this table, COS(90°) is given as .000001 and TAN(90°) = 890059. The correct values for these are 0 and ∞, respectively. These inaccuracies are due to round-off and conversion errors such as those discussed in the next chapter.

EXERCISES

1. Write a BASIC program which will print a table of values in 7 columns for: M, 2M + 6, $(2M+6)^2$, EXP(2M+6), M^3, sine of M radians and the cosine of (10 −M). The value of M should be from 10 to 20 inclusive. Provide appropriate headings.

2. Write a BASIC program which will print a table of values in 7 columns for: an integer X, X^2, X+5, X−5, $(X+5)^2$, EXP(X) and LOG(X). The table should include values of X from 2 to 20 inclusive. Provide appropriate headings.

3. Write out carefully the output produced by a run of the following program. Indicate blank spaces in a line with dashes (-) and blank lines with a plus (+) in the first column.

```
10  J=1
20  FOR I=1 TO 30
30  IF J = 6* INT (J/6) THEN 70
40  J= J +1
50  PRINT "A";
60  GOTO 130
70  J= J+1
80  IF J<25 THEN 120
90  PRINT
100 J=0
110 GOTO 130
120 PRINT
130 NEXT I
140 END
```

Check your results by running the program.

4. Write out carefully the output produced by a run of the following program:

```
100   GO SUB 500
110   FOR I = 1 TO 19
120   IF I = 5*INT(I/5) THEN 150
130   PRINT "."; TAB (I), "X"; SPA(19—I), "."
140   GOTO 160
150   PRINT "+"; TAB (I), "X"; SPA(19—I), "+"
160   NEXT I
170   GO SUB 500
180   STOP
500   FOR I = 1 TO 4
510   PRINT "* . . . . ";
520   NEXT I
530   PRINT "*"
540   RETURN
600   END
```

Verify your result by running the program.

6

Realistic Computing

Up to this point, very little has been said about the restrictions imposed by the computer on our ability to solve problems. In this chapter we shall discuss several sources of errors which occur in most computer applications. We shall also discuss, briefly, the difficulties involved in formulating problems for the computer.

LIMITATIONS OF THE COMPUTER

Round-off Errors

The computer can store and operate on numbers only to a specified accuracy. For example, a typical computer (called "Brand X") has only seven significant figure accuracy. While the discussion here applies to all computers, no matter how many significant figures it carries, "Brand X" is considered as a specific example.

The computer does not round off a number which has more than 7 decimal places; it truncates it; i.e., it throws away all decimal places after the seventh.

Thus, the number

$$12345.6789$$

would be stored as

$$12345.67$$

The .0089 would be discarded.

When printing, the "Brand X" computer rounds numbers to 6 places before printing.

To illustrate the effect this can have, consider a hypothetical computer which has only three decimal place accuracy. (While no computer has only three decimal place accuracy, it is easier to demonstrate the effect of rounding and truncation for such a hypothetical machine.)

If we multiply two numbers

$$5.24 \times 5.24 = 27.4$$

according to the (3 decimal place) computer, the exact value of the product is 27.4576. The last three decimal places (the .0576) are discarded.

Let us now consider the following equation

$$Y = X^3 - 6X^2 + 4X - 0.1$$

and suppose that we wish to evaluate Y at X = 5.24. According to our computer,

$$4X \ = 20.9 \qquad \text{(exact result} = 20.96)$$
$$6X^2 = 164 \qquad \text{(exact result} = 164.7456)$$
$$X^3 \ = 143 \qquad \text{(exact result} = 143.877824)$$

Thus Y = 143. − 164. + 20.9 − 0.100 = −0.200.

The exact result is −0.007776. The answer the 3 place computer gives is not even accurate to 1 significant figure. The problem here is that some of the numbers involved in calculating Y are very large compared to the answer. The 143. and 164. have no significant figures to the right of the decimal point. Since our answer involves fractional numbers, the errors introduced by truncation in calculating the X^3 and $6X^2$ terms are larger than the answer. Thus, it is not surprising that the computer gives us an incorrect answer.

A table illustrating the effect of decimal places carried by the computer for this problem is presented below. The computation is done as above.

Decimal Places Carried	Y
3	−0.200
4	−0.0400
5	−0.01000
7	−0.007800
9	−0.007776

Note that 9 significant figures are required to produce the exact result.

A useful trick for this particular problem is to write

$$Y = ((X - 6)X + 4)X - .1$$

If the calculation is done from the innermost parentheses out, only six decimal places are required to get the exact answer. Factoring polynominals in this manner usually improves the accuracy of the calculation.

To illustrate the kind of difficulties round-off errors can cause, suppose we have some complicated function and wish to calculate numerically the slope of the function at some point, X_*.

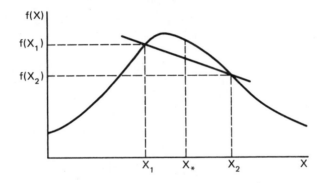

The slope, S, of the line illustrated above is

$$S = \frac{f(X_1) - f(X_2)}{X_1 - X_2}$$

If we let $X_1 = X_*$ and let X_2 approach X_* from the right, we get a better and better approximation to the slope,

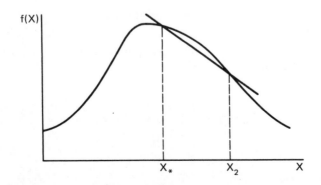

if we view the problem from a purely geometric point of view. From a computer point of view, however, we get an improved estimate of the slope until the round-off errors introduced by subtracting two nearly equal numbers become significant.

To illustrate this idea, let us calculate the slope of Y = SIN(X) at X = 45° ($\pi/4$). The exact answer is 0.707107. In the program below we selected $X_1 = X_*$ and $X_2 = X_* + D$

```
 10  LET X = .785398
 20  LET D = .1
 30  PRINT "D", "SLOPE",
 35  PRINT "-----------------------------------------------"
 40  FOR I = 1 TO 7
 50  LET Y1 = SIN(X+D)
 60  LET Y2 = SIN(X)
 70  LET Y5 = (Y1—Y2)/D
 80  PRINT D, Y5
 90  LET D=D/10
100  NEXT I
110  END
```

The results are summarized in the table below

D	SLOPE
.1	.670602
.01	.703561
.001	.706673
.0001	.706911
.00001	.703335
.000001	.715256
1.00000E—07	1.19209

From the table, it is clear that the best approximation is D = 0.0001. For D smaller than this, round-off errors start to predominate.

This brings us to the important question of how to select D, *a priori* when you are writing a computer program. This question is difficult to answer since there are no general rules one can use. One useful approach is not to select D smaller than is absolutely necessary to obtain results to the required accuracy. Some testing may be needed to select D for any particular problem.

Conversion errors

All computer arithmetic is done in terms of the binary number system rather than the usual decimal number system. The first operation a computer performs is to convert every number given to it into a binary representation.

The binary number system is based on representing numbers as powers of 2 rather than 10, as in our usual decimal number system. For example, the number 25 should be thought of as

$$2 \times 10^1 + 5 \times 10^0$$

We write this as 25 only as a shorthand notation. In binary, this number is thought of as

$$\underline{1} \times 2^4 + \underline{1} \times 2^3 + \underline{0} \times 2^2 + \underline{0} \times 2^1 + \underline{1} \times 2^0$$

or in the same shorthand notation

$$11001$$

The only "digits" in the binary number system are 0 and 1.

The problem for computers comes in the representation of fractions.

For example, 0.25 is thought of as

$$2 \times 10^{-1} + 5 \times 10^{-2}$$

In binary this number is

$$0 \times 2^{-1} + 1 \times 2^{-2}$$

or in the usual (binary) shorthand

$$0.01$$

Some numbers which are convenient in decimal arithmetic are not convenient in binary. For example, 0.1 in decimal is represented as

$$0.00011001100110011 \ldots$$

Thus, 0.1 in decimal is a repeating infinite series in binary. (This is analogous to the impossibility of representing the fraction 1/3 exactly in the decimal system.)

The "Brand X" computer carries 23 "bits" (binary places), which is roughly equivalent to 7 decimal places. To illustrate the problem that can arise, suppose we have a computer that carries only 5 bits. In this hypothetical computer, the decimal number 0.1 would be represented as 0.00011 in binary. This represents

$$0 \times 2^{-1} + 0 \times 2^{-2} + 0 \times 2^{-3} + 1 \times 2^{-4} + 1 \times 2^{-5}$$

or

$$1/16 + 1/32 = 0.09375 \text{ (decimal)}$$

Every computer, no matter how many bits it carries, will always represent 0.1 decimal as a binary number whose decimal equivalent is slightly smaller than 0.1.

This fact is particularly important when comparing two numbers in an IF . . . THEN statement. Consider the following sequence of steps:

```
10  LET D = 0.1
15  LET N = 10
20  LET X = 0.0
30  FOR I = 1 TO N STEP 1
40  LET X = X + D
50  NEXT I
60  IF X = 1 THEN 90
        .
        .
        .
```

The computer converts D to 0.00011 (binary). D gets added to X 10 times in the FOR . . . NEXT loop. If we add 0.00011 (binary) to X 10 times, then when leaving the loop, X = 0.11110 (binary) or 0.9375 (decimal). The value of X is not equal to 1 so the IF . . . THEN relation is not satisfied in line 60. Clearly, if the arithmetic had been done in decimal, the IF . . . THEN relation would have been satisfied. While this problem is exaggerated by our considering a 5 bit computer, this problem could also occur in a 23 bit computer. While this program would run in a 23 bit computer, if we changed D to 0.01 and N = 100, it would not.

There are two tricks for avoiding this problem. One of the tricks is to keep in mind the binary representation of the numbers and use only numbers which can be represented exactly in the number of bits allowed. If we change the above program to

```
10  LET D = 0.125
20  LET X = 0.0
30  FOR I = 1 TO 8 STEP 1
40  LET X = X + D
50  NEXT I
60  IF X = 1 THEN 90
     .
     .
     .
```

we would have no trouble since the binary representation of 0.125 is 0.001 (or 1×2^{-3}).

The other trick is perhaps a little more general. Instead of requiring X to equal 1, require that X be very nearly equal to 1. For our 23 bit computer we could replace the IF . . . THEN statement by

```
60  IF ABS(X − 1) <= 0.00001  THEN 90
```

and avoid the problem. In most real computer programs, this test would determine X accurately enough. The choice of the allowable error (in this case 0.00001) varies from problem to problem. If you are aware of this difficulty, a little experimenting will help you choose the correct factor.

Note that this same effect is present in FOR . . . NEXT statements when the step size is not exactly representable in binary. This can cause the computer to go through the loop one more time than expected.

Round-off and conversion errors generally are cumulative; i.e., the more operations involved in a computer program, the larger the total effect of these two sources of errors. Thus, to minimize the effect of these errors, we should use as few steps as possible. On the other hand, e.g., in our rocket simulation program at the end of Chapter 4, the smaller we make the time increment, I, the more accurate the results. Making I smaller increases the number of steps. Thus we must be careful to make I small enough to get the accuracy we desire yet not so small as to lose that accuracy through round-off and conversion errors.

Truncation Errors

The solutions of many problems involve functions which can be represented as infinite series in powers of their arguments. For example

$$\text{Sin}(X) = X - \frac{X^3}{3!} + \frac{X^5}{5!} - \frac{X^7}{7!} + \frac{X^9}{9!} \ldots$$

Series like this are called Taylor series. While the most important of these functions, e.g., the trigonometric, exponential, and natural logarithm are built in, intrinsic functions, we are often faced with the problem of summing such a series.

To illustrate the difficulty, let us evaluate the SIN using the series for several values of X. If we could sum all the terms (there are an infinute number of them), this series would give the exact value for the SIN for all X. In practice, we can sum only the first few terms. As an example, let us sum only the first five terms (the ones explicitly shown above).

```
For X = .523599          (30°)
SIN(X) = 0.5       SUM OF FIRST 5 TERMS = 0.5

For X = 5.75959          (330°)
SIN (X) = −0.5     SUM OF FIRST 5 TERMS = −4.23679
```

The problem here is that the larger the value of X, the more terms in the series must be kept in order to achieve a given accuracy. For 30°, five terms in the series was adequate; but for 330°, five terms was not adequate.

The error introduced by keeping too few terms is called truncation error.

One commonly used technique for avoiding this problem is to continue adding terms until the sum does not change significantly. The following program illustrates this technique:

```
10  REM: PROGRAM TO SUM SINE SERIES
20  PRINT "INPUT X IN RADIANS"
30  INPUT X
40  LET S = 0
50  LET N = 1
```

```
 70  LET T = X
 80  LET S = S + T
 90  IF ABS(T/S)<1.E − 07 THEN 130
100  LET N = N + 2
110  LET T = −T∗X↑2/(N∗(N−1))
120  GO TO 80
130  PRINT "SIN(X) = "; S
140  GO TO 20
150  END
```

This is a rather efficient algorithm for summing the sine series. Each term in the series is computed from the previous term by multiplying by $-X{\uparrow}2/(N*(N-1))$. This has the real advantage of avoiding the calculation of $X{\uparrow}N$ and N! for each term.

If N! had to be calculated for each term, only a limited number of terms could be calculated since N! would soon be too large for the computer to handle. For many computers, the largest number which can be handled is 10^{38}. A few will handle much larger numbers. Note that $N! > 10^{38}$ for $N > 34$.

This program will not work for all X since the larger X gets, the more terms are needed in the sum. For example, for X=9, 37 terms are required, and round-off errors start to appear in the fourth significant figure.

For the intrinsic function SIN(X), the computer does not use a series solution. The intrinsic function works for any value of X.

The purpose of this program is to illustrate a general technique for summing series. If we were serious about summing the SIN series, we would take advantage of its periodicity and add the statement

```
35  LET X = X −2 ∗ 3.14159 ∗ INT (X/(2 ∗ 3.14159)) + 0.5)
```

since SIN $(2\pi K + X) = $ SIN(X) for any integer K. Now this program would work for all X. Unfortunately, most series we wish to sum do not have the periodicity of the SIN.

Most problems require some approximations in order to be suitable for solution on the computer. The truncation problem is only one example. Generally speaking, this is the most difficult part of solving problems on the computer. In a later chapter, we shall present some numerical techniques for solving some common problems and, at that time, we shall return to this question.

COMPUTER TIME

The amount of time it takes the computer to run your program depends on many factors and is quite complicated. There is one point, however, that should be made. The teletype terminal, for example, prints 10 characters per second. There are other terminals which print much faster, but these are not as commonly used.

Since the teletype line has 72 characters it takes 7.2 seconds for each line printed. In many programs, this is the factor which controls the speed at which your program is run.

If, for example, in the rocket simulation program we had printed out the results every second instead of every 10 seconds, it would have taken approximately 1 hour to print out.

It is important to take care not to generate excessive print out. In those cases when a large amount of print out is necessary you should consider using a "Line Printer" if one is available. Line printers generally print 200 or more lines/minute. For the rocket example, the line printer would print the results for every second in approximately 3 minutes. See the user's manual for instructions.

DEBUGGING

The term debugging refers to removing errors in a computer program. These errors can be either syntax (language) errors or logic errors. The computer checks the program for syntax errors and prints out error messages. Logical errors are much more difficult to identify as they usually show up in the form of incorrect answers.

There are a number of steps that you can take to reduce the number of errors you make and to speed up the process of eliminating them.

First, write the program in short segments and debug each segment as you proceed. The longer the program, the harder it is to isolate the problem.

Second, print out intermediate results especially in problem areas. Don't assume that a particular variable has a particular value because you think it must. Print it out. Add print statements with comments to indicate which path the computer took through the program.

For example, selected lines from a program might look like

.
.
.

150 LET S = 6

.
.
.

260 LET A = 8

.
.
.

840 FOR I = 1 TO 8
850 LET T(I) = S + I ↑ A
860 NEXT I

.
.
.

9999 END

When you ran the program, the computer responded with an error message

UNDEFINED VALUE ASSESSED IN LINE 850

Looking briefly at the program doesn't reveal the problem so add the following two lines:

151 PRINT "CHECK POINT #1"
261 PRINT "CHECK POINT #2"

Now running the program produces

CHECK POINT #1
UNDEFINED VALUE ASSESSED IN LINE 850

Thus the problem is that the computer is not executing line 260 but is executing line 150. The problem has now been localized and close examination reveals that the trouble is in line 240 which reads

240 IF S = 6 THEN 840

Thus the "bug" has now been located and can be corrected in an appropriate way.

Perhaps the most important technique in debugging is to "play computer"—that is follow through the segment of the program that you are writing, step by step exactly as the computer would, comparing your results with the intermediate print out. For this purpose it is often best to choose the data so that the calculations are as simple as possible.

Whenever possible, run a "test case"—that is, a set of data for which you can compute the final result. While this is not always possible, it is an extremely useful debugging tool. Whenever you write a program always try to invent a "test case."

EXERCISES

1. Write a program in BASIC to calculate

$$\log_e \left[\frac{1+X}{1-X} \right] = 2 \left[X + \frac{X^3}{3} + \frac{X^5}{5} + \dots \frac{X^{2n-1}}{2n-1} \right]$$

by summing the series. This series holds for $(-1<X<1)$. The program should accept a value of X and make sure that it is in the proper range. Include additional terms in the series until the last term changes the sum by less than 0.1% of the previous sum.

2. Write a program in BASIC to calculate

$$\log_e (1 + X) = X - \frac{X^2}{2} + \frac{X^3}{3} - \frac{X^4}{4} + \dots \frac{X^n}{n}$$

by summing the series. This series holds for $(-1 < X < 1)$. The program should accept values of X and check to make sure that it is in the appropriate range. Include additional terms in the series until the last term is less than 1% of the computed answer.

Check your answer by computing $\log_e (1 + X)$ using the intrinsic function.

3. The infinite series representation of e^x is

$$\exp (x) = 1 + x + \frac{x^2}{2!} + \frac{x^3}{3!} + \dots$$

For practical purposes one can use a finite number of terms and truncate the series when adding one more term causes the value of e^x to change by less than some percent, D, from its previous value.

Write a program to calculate exp(x) for $x = -0.5, -1, -2, -6,$ $+6$ when $D = 10^{-4}$ and 10^{-6}. Compare the values so obtained with the value of exp(x) using the computer function. Print out all results in a table including the number of terms in the series required in each case.

4. Using the LOG function on the computer, obtain the values of log $(1 + x)$ where $x = 10^{-1}$, 10^{-3} and 10^{-7}. The correct values to six digits are, respectively, 0.095310, 9.99950×10^{-4} and 1.00000×10^{-7}.

    Explain why the results obtained from the computer do not agree with the accurate values.

5. Write a program that calculates the square roots of all integers between 1 and 500 and prints only those roots which are integers. Calculate the square root both by using SQR and by raising to the 1/2 power.

    a) What conclusion(s) can you draw about the relative accuracy of the SQR function and raising to a power?

    b) What conclusion(s) can you draw about how to test for a number being an integer? About testing whether two numbers are equal?

7

Matrices

In Chapter 2, we saw that variable names were not restricted to letters or letters followed by a single digit. In fact, subscripted variables provide a great deal of added flexibility. The singly-subscripted variables, called lists or vectors, or arrays, provided a way to change variable names dynamically within the program. This is of great benefit when it is desirable to perform the same series of operations on each element in a list of data.

The BASIC language provides another degree of flexibility through the use of doubly-subscripted variables, called tables or matrices or arrays. To illustrate how these are used, consider the following example:

In a class of 5 students, each student turns in 6 homework assignments. On each assignment he gets a grade between 0 and 10. We put these numbers in a table where the rows of the table represent the students, and the columns, the grades on each homework assignment.

	Homework 1	Homework 2	Homework 3	Homework 4	Homework 5	Homework 6
Student 1	6	5	7	8	4	3
Student 2	9	10	9	9	8	7
Student 3	4	8	6	5	9	8
Student 4	7	9	9	8	9	8
Student 5	8	8	7	9	8	8

We could store these numbers in the computer in the form of a doubly-subscripted variable or array.

Let $S(1,1), S(1,2), \ldots S(1,6), S(2,1), \ldots S(5,1), S(5,2), \ldots S(5,6)$, be our array. Here the first number or subscript in the parentheses refers to the row (or student in this example) and the second subscript to the column (or homework assignment). Variables can be used for subscripts; for example, if $I = 5$ and $J = 3$, then $S(I,J)$ refers to the grade for student 5 on homework assignment 3.

In order to use an array in a computer program, we must first reserve storage space for it by telling the computer the maximum number of rows and columns in the array. This is done by using a DIM (dimension) statement. Thus

```
10   DIM S(5,6)
```

reserves room in storage for an array S with 5 rows and 6 columns (30 elements in all).

More than one array can be "DIMensioned" in a DIM statement. For example,

```
10   DIM S(5,6), T(18), F(7,4)
```

As indicated in Chapter 2, an array name may be any single letter, thus allowing only 26 possible names.

The following program could be used to compute each student's average for the homework and the class average for each homework

```
10   DIM S(5,6), A(5), H(6)
20   FOR I=1 TO 5
30   FOR J=1 TO 6
40   READ S(I, J)
50   NEXT J
60   NEXT I
70   REM: COMPUTE STUDENTS AVERAGE, A
80   FOR I=1 TO 5
90   LET A(I)=0
100  FOR J=1 TO 6
110  LET A(I)=A(I) + S(I,J)/6
120  NEXT J
130  PRINT "AVERAGE FOR STUDENT"; I; "="; A(I)
140  NEXT I
150  PRINT
160  REM: COMPUTE AVERAGE FOR EACH HOMEWORK
```

```
170  FOR J=1 TO 6
180  LET H(J)=0
190  FOR I=1 TO 5
200  LET H(J)=H(J)+S(I,J)/5
210  NEXT I
220  PRINT "AVERAGE FOR HOMEWORK ";J;"=";H(J)
230  NEXT J
240  DATA 6, 5, 7, 8, 4, 3
250  DATA 9, 10, 9, 9, 8, 7
260  DATA 4, 8, 6, 5, 9, 8
270  DATA 7, 9, 9, 8, 9, 8
280  DATA 8, 8, 7, 9, 8, 8
290  END
```

Note that lines 20-60 read in S(I,J) row by row.

Sometimes we will refer to S(I,J) and imply that we are referring to some arbitrary element in the array. It should be understood that I and J must be specified before this statement has real meaning.

Of course, I and J must be integers since they refer to rows and columns. We can replace them by expressions such as

$$S(I+4, J-5)$$

If the values of the expressions are not integers, the computer rounds to the nearest integer.

Many common operations on Matrices have been made part of the BASIC language. These operations can simplify the computer program significantly.

For the remainder of this chapter, we will refer to singly-subscripted variables as vectors and doubly-subscripted variables as matrices.

For most MAT statements which we are about to discuss, the indicated operation can be performed on either vectors or matrices. In these cases, we should think of a vector as a matrix with only 1 column.[†]

We will use the word "array" as a general term to mean either a vector or a matrix when either one can be used.

[†] These are sometimes called column vectors. Matrices with only 1 row are sometimes called row vectors. Singly-subscripted variables are treated by the computer as column vectors. Thus row vectors must be dimensioned as 10 DIM S (I,N). When used in these notes, the term vector will refer to a column vector.

MAT READ

In the example above, lines 20 through 60 did nothing more than read in the matrix S, row by row. The equivalent MAT operation is

20 MAT READ S

This statement performs exactly the same operations as lines 20-60.

Since S was dimensioned S(5,6), the MAT READ statement reads 6 numbers into each of 5 rows, filling one row at a time.

A vector can be read in the same manner. If X is a vector, then

10 DIM X(6)
20 MAT READ X
30 DATA 1, 3, 4, 2, 8, 5

will read the 6 values in the DATA statement into the vector X.

For convenience, we will write the vector X in the following form

$$X = \begin{bmatrix} X(1) \\ X(2) \\ X(3) \\ X(4) \\ X(5) \\ X(6) \end{bmatrix}$$

In this case

$$X = \begin{bmatrix} 1 \\ 3 \\ 4 \\ 2 \\ 8 \\ 5 \end{bmatrix}$$

You can read in more than one array at a time with a single MAT READ statement simply by separating them with commas. Thus, if you have DIM statements like

```
10   DIM S (4,4)
20   DIM A(2,3), B(3,4)
```

these arrays can be read using a single statement

```
30   MAT READ A, B, S
```

In this statement, A is read row by row. Then B is read in row by row until it is complete. Finally, S is read.

If these statements appeared in a program with DATA statements like

```
100   DATA  1, 2, 3, 4, 5, 6, 7, 8
110   DATA  9, 10, 11, 12, 13, 14, 15, 16
120   DATA  17, 18, 19, 20, 21, 22, 23, 24
130   DATA  25, 26, 27, 28, 29, 30, 31, 32
140   DATA  33, 34
```

the result would be:

$$A = \begin{bmatrix} 1 & 2 & 3 \\ 4 & 5 & 6 \end{bmatrix}$$

$$B = \begin{bmatrix} 7 & 8 & 9 & 10 \\ 11 & 12 & 13 & 14 \\ 15 & 16 & 17 & 18 \end{bmatrix}$$

and

$$S = \begin{bmatrix} 19 & 20 & 21 & 22 \\ 23 & 24 & 25 & 26 \\ 27 & 28 & 29 & 30 \\ 31 & 32 & 33 & 34 \end{bmatrix}$$

Note that care must be taken to put the data for the various matrix elements in the proper place in the DATA statement.

MAT INPUT

The MAT INPUT works essentially the same way as the MAT READ. The statements

```
10  DIM  A(2,3)
20  MAT  INPUT A
```

would cause a "?" to be printed and you would respond with the values of the elements of A. These values would have to be entered row by row, separated by commas, until A was entirely filled.

For large arrays, not all elements can be typed on the same line. For this case, type in as many as you like on the line and depress the return. The computer will continue to accept values until enough have been entered to assign one value to each element in A.

If more than one array appears in the MAT INPUT statement, the first array is filled completely, row by row, then the second array, and so on.

MAT PRINT

The MAT PRINT statement causes the computer to print the arrays row by row. Each row starts a new line and is separated from previous rows by a blank line. If a row contains more elements than can be printed on a line, the computer goes to the next line and continues printing the row.

```
10  DIM  A(5,6)
20  FOR I=1 TO 5
30  FOR J=1 TO 6
40  LET  A(I,J) = (I+J)
50  NEXT J
60  NEXT I
70  MAT PRINT A
80  END
```

will produce

2	3	4	5	6
7				
3	4	5	6	7
8				
4	5	6	7	8
9				
5	6	7	8	9
10				
6	7	8	9	10
11				

More than one array can be printed in a MAT PRINT statement. For example

```
10  MAT PRINT A, B, F
```

would result in A being printed completely, then B, then F.

Spacing between elements in a row can be controlled using commas and semi-colons. A comma prints 5 elements to a line and a semi-colon up to 12, following the rules for printing ordinary variables. Thus,

```
10  MAT PRINT A, B; F;
```

would print A, five elements to a line, and B and F would be printed in the "packed" format. The dangling semi-colon only indicates that F is printed according to the rules for printing variables using semi-colons. The carriage return and line-feed are not affected.

MULTIPLYING AN ARRAY BY A CONSTANT

We can multiply each element in an array by the same number in the following manner

```
 5  DIM  A(3,4), B(3,4)
10  MAT A = (6) * B
```

Statement 10 multiplies each element in the array B by 6 and stores it in the corresponding element in A. This is equivalent to

```
10  FOR F=1 TO 3
20  FOR K=1 TO 4
30  LET A(F,K)=6*B(F,K)
40  NEXT K
50  NEXT F
```

We may multiply each element in an array by any legitimate BASIC expression. The expression must be put in parentheses. Thus, statement 10 above could be

$$10 \quad MAT \ A = (A1 + B9)*B$$

provided A1 and B9 had been assigned values.

The dimensions of the two arrays (A and B) must be the same in a statement of this type.

The same array can be used on both sides of the assignment operator as in

$$10 \quad MAT \ A = (C1)*A$$

For this case, each element is multiplied by C1 and the result is stored again in the array A.

A single letter, such as A or B, can be used both as a variable name and as an array name. This will not confuse the computer since it will assume that the letter A or B, for example, is an array when it appears in MAT statements. Any other time that this letter appears in any other kind of statement, the computer will assume that it is a simple variable. While the use of the same single letter for both a simple variable name and an array name will not confuse the computer, it may confuse the programmer. For example, the statements

```
10  DIM A(3,4), B(3,4)
15  MAT B=CON
20  LET A=5
30  LET B=4
40  MAT A= (A+B)*B
```

are perfectly legal. Each element in the array B will be multiplied by 9 and stored in the array A.

The confusion this can cause is obvious and the practice should be avoided.

MAT ADDITION AND SUBTRACTION

Matrices can be added or subtracted by using statements of the form

```
10  DIM A(5,6), D(5,6), G(5,6)
20  MAT A= D+G
30  MAT D= G—A
```

Statement 30 is equivalent to

```
30  FOR K= 1 TO 5
40  FOR L= 1 TO 6
50  LET D(K,L) = G(K,L) — A(K,L)
60  NEXT L
70  NEXT K
```

In statement 30 above, each element of A is subtracted from the corresponding element in G and the result is assigned to the corresponding element of D. Addition works in a completely analogous manner. All of the three arrays in a "MAT add" or "MAT subtract" statement must have the same dimensions.

Only one operation is allowed in each MAT statement. Thus

```
10  DIM A(5,6), F(5,6), M(5,6), H(5,6)
20  MAT  A = (3.1)∗ F—M
```

is not allowed.

The operations indicated in statement 20 can be accomplished in two steps as follows

```
20  MAT  H= (3.1)∗ F
30  MAT  A= H—M
```

The statement

```
20  MAT  A= F+M—H
```

is also illegal. We must accomplish this in two steps

```
20  MAT  A= F+M
30  MAT  A= A—H
```

SPECIAL MATRICES

There are several special arrays that are very helpful. One of these is the zero array in which each element is zero. To set all the elements equal to zero in any array, we can use a statement like

10 MAT A=ZER

The array A must, of course, be dimensioned beforehand.

Another useful array is one in which all elements are 1. This can be accomplished using

10 MAT A= CON

This statement sets all elements of A equal to 1. Again, A must be dimensioned first.

A square matrix is one in which the number of rows equals the number of columns. The diagonal of a square matrix refers to the elements along the diagonal line from upper left to lower right. For example,

$$\begin{bmatrix} D & N & N \\ N & D & N \\ N & N & D \end{bmatrix}$$

The D's are the diagonal elements and the N's are nondiagonal elements.

One important square matrix is the identity matrix which has all 1's on the diagonal and zeros elsewhere. Thus

$$\begin{bmatrix} 1 & 0 & 0 \\ 0 & 1 & 0 \\ 0 & 0 & 1 \end{bmatrix}$$

is an example of an identity matrix.

An identity matrix can be generated with a statement like

10 MAT A= IDN

The number of rows in A must be equal to the number of columns. If A had been dimensioned A(3,3) a matrix like the above would have been created.

SAMPLE PROGRAM

In the example presented in the beginning of this chapter, we defined a matrix, S, where the rows represented students and the columns grades (based on 10 possible points) on homework. Thus, $S(3,6) =$ grade on homework 6 by student 3.

The following program will calculate a matrix, P, which represents the percent missed by each student on each homework. Thus, $S(3,6) = 8$, so $P(3,6) = 20$ (percent).

```
10  DIM P(5,6), S(5,6), C(5,6)
20  REM:  READ IN GRADES ROW BY ROW
30  MAT  READ S
40  REM:  C=POSSIBLE SCORES
50  MAT  C=CON
60  MAT  C=(10)*C
70  MAT  P=C-S
80  REM:  CONVERT TO PERCENT
90  MAT  P=(10)*P
100  PRINT "TABLE OF PERCENT MISSED ON HOMEWORK"
110  MAT  PRINT P;
120  DATA  6, 5, 7, 8, 4, 3, 9, 10, 9, 9, 8, 7
130  DATA  4, 8, 6, 5, 9, 8, 7, 9, 9, 8, 9, 8
140  DATA  8, 8, 7, 9, 8, 8
150  END
```

MULTIPLICATION OF TWO ARRAYS

Two arrays can be multiplied provided that the number of columns of the first array is equal to the number of rows in the second. The product is an array with the number of rows equal to the number of rows of the first array and the number of columns equal to the number of columns in the second array.

Thus, if A is dimensioned A(3,4) and B is dimensioned B(4,2), then the product A*B is an array with 3 rows and 2 columns. Thus, if we dimension C(3,2), then we can write

$$10 \quad MAT\ C = A*B$$

where C is defined as

$$C(I, J) = \sum_{K=1}^{4} A(I, K)*B(K, J)$$

for $1 \leqslant I \leqslant 3$ and $1 \leqslant J \leqslant 2$.

We cannot, for this case, define B*A since the number of columns of B is not equal to the number of rows of A. In general A*B $\neq$ B*A even if both products are defined.

For example, if A is dimensioned A(2,3), B dimensioned B(3,2) and C dimensioned C(2,2) and

$$A = \begin{bmatrix} 2 & 1 & 4 \\ 3 & 2 & 5 \end{bmatrix} \quad \text{and} \quad B = \begin{bmatrix} 1 & 5 \\ 2 & 1 \\ 3 & -2 \end{bmatrix}$$

Then

$$C = A*B = \begin{bmatrix} 16 & 3 \\ 22 & 7 \end{bmatrix}$$

Since $C(1,1) = 2 \cdot 1 + 1 \cdot 2 + 4 \cdot 3 = 16$, $C(1,2) = 2 \cdot 5 + 1 \cdot 1 + 4 \cdot (-2) = 3$, $C(2,1) = 3 \cdot 1 + 2 \cdot 2 + 5 \cdot 3 = 22$, and $C(2,2) = 3 \cdot 5 + 2 \cdot 1 + 5 \cdot (-2) = 7$.

A vector with N elements can be thought of as matrix with N rows and 1 column. Thus, if X is a vector with three elements we can think of it as

$$X = \begin{bmatrix} 6 \\ 9 \\ -2 \end{bmatrix}$$

and

$$D = A*X = \begin{bmatrix} 13 \\ 26 \end{bmatrix}$$

Here D must be dimensioned D(2) (or D(2,1)).
The computer performs these operations with the single statement

```
10  DIM A(2,3), B(3,2), C(2,2)
20  MAT C = A*B
```

Note that the dimensions of A, B, and C must satisfy the rules given above. Also, in a MAT multiplication, an array may <u>not</u> appear on both sides of the assignment operation.

LINEAR EQUATIONS

Let us consider the problem of solving two equations in two unknowns.

$$A(1,1) \; X(1) + A(1,2) \; X(2) = B(1)$$
$$A(2,1) \; X(1) + A(2,2) \; X(2) = B(2)$$

(1)

Here, X(1) and X(2) are the unknowns and the coefficients (assume specified) are stored in the array A. For example,

$$X(1) - 2X(2) = -3$$
$$2X(1) + X(2) = 4$$

(2)

So, A(1,1) = 1, A(1,2) = −2, A(2,1) = 2, A(2,2) = 1, B(1) = −3, and B(2) = 4.

To solve these equations on the computer, we must consider the left-hand side as the product of two arrays, A and X. In matrix notations we write

$$A*X = B$$

(3)

where the product A*X is interpreted exactly as the left hand side of (1) above.

Note that we can interpret this as a vector with elements

$$A(1,1)*X(1) + A(1,2)*X(2)$$
$$A(2,1)*X(1) + A(2,2)*X(2)$$

We cannot yet solve these equations because there is no "matrix division" operation. There are matrix techniques for solving these equations which we will get to shortly. First, however, we must again discuss the identity matrix.

THE IDENTITY MATRIX

The identity matrix was defined as a square matrix (number of rows = number of columns) with 1's on the diagonal and 0's everywhere else.

Let I be the identify matrix dimensioned I(3,3) and consider I*X. It is easy to see that

$$I*X = X$$

and

$$I*B = B$$

and

$$A*I = A$$

In fact, the product of the identity matrix with any matrix leaves the other matrix unchanged.

Thus to solve the linear equations

$$A*X = B \tag{3}$$

we would like to find a matrix, D, such that

$$D*A = I$$

Then if we multiply (3) by D we get

$$D*A*X = D*B$$

or

$$I*X = D*B$$

or

$$X = D*B$$

D is called the inverse of A (sometimes written as A^{-1}). Only square arrays can have inverses. This implies that the number of equations equals the number of unknowns. Not all square arrays do have inverses; if the set of equations (1) has a unique solution, then the array has an inverse, otherwise A does not have an inverse.

One way to find the inverse of an array is to solve the set of equations. For the example above, write

$$X(1) - 2X(2) = B(1)$$
$$2X(1) + X(2) = B(2)$$

Then

$$X(1) = \frac{B(1)}{5} + \frac{2B(2)}{5}$$

$$X(2) = \frac{-2B(1)}{5} + \frac{B(2)}{5}$$

Thus, the inverse D of A where

$$A = \begin{bmatrix} 1 & -2 \\ 2 & 1 \end{bmatrix} \quad \text{is} \quad D = \begin{bmatrix} 1/5 & 2/5 \\ -2/5 & 1/5 \end{bmatrix}$$

Note that

$$D * A = A * D = \begin{bmatrix} 1 & 0 \\ 0 & 1 \end{bmatrix}$$

the identity matrix. The computer can find the inverse of a matrix, A, using the following statement

```
10   DIM A(2,2), D(2,2)
15   MAT READ A
20   MAT D = INV(A)
```

If the set of equations corresponding to the array A does not have a unique solution, then D will not exist; and the computer will respond to line 20 with a diagnostic message NEARLY SINGULAR MATRIX.

SAMPLE PROGRAM

The following program will solve a set of three equations in three un-knowns. (To solve more equations in more unknowns, simply change the dimension statement and data.)

```
 10  REM:  LINEAR EQUATIONS PROGRAM
 20  DIM A (3,3), B(3), X(3), D(3,3)
 30  REM:  READ COEFFICIENT MATRIX, A AND CONSTANTS, B
 40  MAT  READ A, B
 50  MAT D=INV(A)
 60  MAT X=D*B
 70  PRINT "SOLUTION OF EQUATIONS"
 80  MAT PRINT X
 90  DATA 1, −2, 2
100  DATA 2, 1, −1
110  DATA 1, −2, 3
120  DATA 3, 1, 6
130  END
```

This data corresponds to

$$x - 2y + 2z = 3$$
$$2x + y - z = 1$$
$$x - 2y + 3z = 6$$

Running this program with this data results in

SOLUTION OF EQUATIONS

$\underline{1}$

$\underline{2}$

$\underline{3}$

As a further example, consider the following set of equations:

$$3A + B - 2C + D = 5$$
$$A + 2C - 4 = 5B$$
$$A + B = C + D$$
$$3B + 2D = -1$$

The first thing we must do is rewrite these equations so that each unknown (A, B, C or D) is in the same column and all the constants are on the right hand side.

$$3A + B - 2C + D = 5$$
$$A - 5B + 2C + 0D = 4$$
$$A + B - C - D = 0$$
$$0A + 3B + 0C + 2D = -1$$

The coefficient matrix becomes

$$\begin{bmatrix} 3 & 1 & -2 & 1 \\ 1 & -5 & 2 & 0 \\ 1 & 1 & -1 & -1 \\ 0 & 3 & 0 & 2 \end{bmatrix}$$

and the constant matrix becomes

$$\begin{bmatrix} 5 \\ 4 \\ 0 \\ -1 \end{bmatrix}$$

The following program solves these equations.

```
10  REM: PROGRAM FOR FOUR LINEAR EQUATIONS
20  DIM A(4,4), B(4), X(4), D(4,4)
30  REM: READ IN COEFFICIENTS AND CONSTANTS
40  MAT READ A, B
50  MAT D=INV(A)
60  MAT X=D*B
70  PRINT "SOLUTION OF EQUATIONS"
80  MAT PRINT X
90  DATA 3, 1, -2, 1
100 DATA 1, -5, 2, 0
110 DATA 1, 1, -1, -1
120 DATA 0, 3, 0, 2
130 DATA 5, 4, 0, -1
140 END
```

RUN
SOLUTION OF EQUATIONS

1.

-1.

-1.

1

MAT TRANSPOSE

Occasionally, it is useful to transpose the rows and columns of an array. For example, if A is

$$\begin{bmatrix} 1 & 2 \\ 4 & 6 \\ 5 & 8 \end{bmatrix}$$

the transpose of A is (A^T)

$$\begin{bmatrix} 1 & 4 & 5 \\ 2 & 6 & 8 \end{bmatrix}$$

This can be done with MAT statements as follows

```
10  DIM A(3,2), D(2,3)
20  MAT D = TRN(A)
```

Note that the number of rows of D must equal the number of columns of A and the number of columns of D must equal the number of rows of A.

EXERCISES

1. Consider the following two matrices

$$A = \begin{bmatrix} 1 & 7.2 & 3 \\ 2.1 & 9 & 1 \end{bmatrix} \qquad B = \begin{bmatrix} 3 & 8.4 & 9.2 \\ 6 & 5.3 & 7 \end{bmatrix}$$

   a) Add these matrices.
   b) Subtract these matrices.
   c) Multiply the matrix A by the number 5.8.

   Write a program in BASIC, using MAT statements to perform the same operations. Run the program and check your answers.

2. Repeat problem 1 for

$$A = \begin{bmatrix} 1 & 7 & 3 \\ 2 & 8 & 9 \\ 1 & 6 & 4 \end{bmatrix} \qquad \text{and} \qquad B = \begin{bmatrix} 3 & 8 & 1 \\ 2 & 5 & 7 \\ 9 & 2 & 1 \end{bmatrix}$$

3. Consider the following two matrices:

$$A = \begin{bmatrix} 3.1 & 2.6 & 5 \\ 4 & 2 & 8 \end{bmatrix} \quad \text{and} \quad B = \begin{bmatrix} 8 & 1 \\ 6 & 5 \\ 1 & 1 \end{bmatrix}$$

Which product exists?

   i) A*B
  ii) B*A
 iii) both A*B and B*A

Calculate by hand the product(s) which exist(s). Write a program in BASIC using MAT statements to repeat your calculations.

4. Repeat problem 3 with

$$A = \begin{bmatrix} 1 & 8 & 6 & 4 \\ 2 & 1 & 9 & 3 \end{bmatrix} \quad \text{and} \quad B = \begin{bmatrix} 1 & 3 & 4 \\ 2 & 7 & 9 \\ 1 & 6 & 8 \\ 4 & 5 & 1 \end{bmatrix}$$

5. Show that B is the inverse of A where

$$A = \begin{bmatrix} 2 & 1 \\ 1 & 1 \end{bmatrix} \quad \text{and} \quad B = \begin{bmatrix} 1 & -1 \\ -1 & 2 \end{bmatrix}$$

Show that A is the inverse of B.

6. Play computer and write out what you think would be the output of the BASIC program shown below. Run the program and check your results.

```
 20  DIM S(8,11)
 30  MAT S=CON
 40  FOR J= 3 TO 5
 50  FOR M=2 TO 8 STEP 2
 60  LET S(J,M)=J—M
 70  NEXT M
 80  NEXT J
 90  MAT S=(3)*S
100  PRINT S(6,3), S(3,4)
110  END
```

7. Write a BASIC program that will solve the following set of equations and print out the results (none of the matrices are singular):

$$10x_1 + 9x_4 + 21 = 2x_1 + 6x_2 + x_3 + 4x_5$$
$$x_1 + 5x_2 + 2x_5 = 31 + 3x_4$$
$$x_5 + 2 = 2x_2 + 7x_3$$
$$3x_2 + 4x_3 + 19x_4 = 47 + 5x_1$$
$$7x_4 + 9x_5 + 7 = x_3 + 10x_1 + 40$$

8. Which of the following BASIC statements are correct? For the incorrect ones, show how to accomplish the intended operations.

```
10  MAT READ R
20  MAT C = IDN
30  LET J = Q(3,5)+(Q(3,3)↑6)* R(1,5) +7
40  FOR I = R(12) TO R(11) STEP 3*R(6)
70  MAT K =K*R
80  MAT K = Q+R—S
90  MAT N(5,5) = ZER
```

9. Play computer and write out what you think would be the output of the BASIC program below.

```
 20  DIM J(3,5), K(5,3)
 30  MAT J=CON
 40  FOR L=1 TO 5 STEP 2
 50  FOR M=1 TO 3
 60  LET J(M,L)=L*M
 70  NEXT M
 80  NEXT L
 90  MAT K= TRN(J)
100  PRINT K(2,3), J(1,2)
110  END
```

10. Write a program in BASIC that will fill a 6X6 array with odd integers selected at random from the interval —5 to +5 inclusive. The program should print out the resulting array together with the positions in the array at which the smallest integer occurs. (Note that the smallest integer may be greater than —5 and may appear in several positions.)

11. Which of the following statements are correct? How would you replace the incorrect statements? (Note: assume that all matrices are appropriately dimensioned.)

```
10  MAT A =3*B
20  DIM B(25,25), K(5,7)
30  MAT S= S + R(5,6)
40  MAT U = (4*A+B)*V
50  MAT C=(3)*INV(U)
60  MAT J=R(5,6)*S(4,2)+S
```

12. Matrix Z is an N×N matrix which is purported to be the inverse of an N×N matrix A. Write a <u>subroutine</u> in BASIC to determine that matrix Z is indeed the inverse of matrix A. In making the comparison, be certain to account for inherent computer inaccuracies. Assume that N has been specified previously in the program and that all of the elements of the matrices A and Z have also been specified. Hint: A^{-1} *A= Identity Matrix. Test your program.

13. The National Football League wants a computer program in BASIC which sets up an internal table of information. The table (called T in the program) contains a row for each of N running backs (numbered 1 through N), and a column for each of G games (numbered 1 through G). The intersection of a row and a column contains the number of yards gained by that particular player (row number) for that particular game (column number). In addition the program should scan the complete above-mentioned table and determine which, if any, players gained 1000 or more total yards after all G games have been played. The program should cause the computer to print one of the following responses:

a) If no players gain 1000 or more total yards, the computer should print: NO O. J. SIMPSONS HERE!

b) If any player gains 1000 or more total yards, the computer should print the player's number (row number) and the total number of yards he has gained. This applies only to those players who have gained 1000 or more total yards.

14. Write a program in BASIC which will solve the following set of equations and print the values of A, B, C, and D.

$$A - B + 2C + 2D = 1$$
$$A - C - 3D - 6 \ \ = 6$$
$$3A + 2B + 3C + D = 4$$
$$A + B = -C - D$$

15. If A is a matrix and C is a column vector of all ones, then A*C is a vector consisting of the row-sums of A. Using MAT instructions write as short a program as possible to compute and print the row-sums of a given matrix.

16. Write a program in BASIC that will construct an NXN matrix for which the diagonal elements have the value 2 and all other elements have the value 1 and will invert the matrix. Run the program for several values of N. See if you can infer the form of the inverse matrix for arbitrary N.

17. Given an NXN matrix M, write a program in BASIC that tests whether the inverse of M is equal to the transpose of M, i.e., is $M^{-1} = M^T$? (Such a matrix is called an orthogonal matrix.) In making such a test, be sure to account for round-off error.

18. Write a program that will solve the following set of equations and print the values of A, B, C, and D.

$$A + 3B + C - 2D = 5$$
$$2B - C + D - 2A - 2 = 0$$
$$-2B + 2C - D = -1 - 2A$$
$$A - 2C + 3 = 3(B + D)$$

19. A school district has three schools, each one of which has four classes. Write a program which sets up a table of each day of attendance and compares it with a table of enrollment. Print out the number of students absent in each class.

8

Numerical Methods

The previous chapters have been devoted to writing computer programs without really being concerned with how to solve particular problems. In this chapter, some useful techniques for solving a number of problems will be presented along with some more examples.

The techniques chosen for presentation in this chapter are the easiest ones to understand. Generally speaking, they are not the most efficient. However, these methods do work and are useful. In most computer facilities, other more efficient methods are available for general use.

ROOT FINDING

One common problem which occurs in many fields involves finding the solution of an equation of the general form

$$f(x) = 0 \qquad\qquad (1)$$

(Such a solution is called a root or, sometimes, a zero of the function.)
For example, if

$$f(x) = \text{Tan}(x) - 1$$

then a solution of this equation for $0 \leqslant x \leqslant \pi/2$ is $x = \pi/4$.

The problem can be stated in other ways. For example, find the value of x such that

$$e^x = 3.5$$

In this case,

$$f(x) = e^x - 3.5$$

and the solution is

$$x = \log (3.5) = 1.25276$$

There are many methods that can be used for solving problems of this kind. The method presented here is perhaps the simplest; but it is not the most efficient or the most general. The method requires that we be able to guess from the statement of the problem, a value x_1 and a value x_2 such that the solution of eq. (1) lies between x_1 and x_2. For convenience, assume $x_2 > x_1$. This means simply that the signs of $f(x_1)$ and $f(x_2)$ must be different.

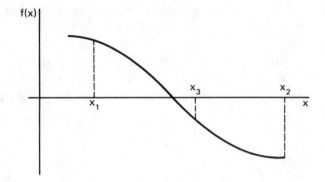

The idea is to halve the interval (x_1, x_2) by finding a value, x_3, where $x_3 = (x_1 + x_2)/2$. We then check to see if the value of $f(x_3)$ is zero within an error limit, E. If it is not, we check to see which interval (x_1, x_3) or (x_3, x_2) contains the solution, i.e., in which interval does f change signs. Suppose for this example that the sign of $f(x_1)$ is different from the sign of $f(x_3)$. (This indicates that the solution lies between x_1 and x_3.) We then halve the interval (x_1, x_3) and proceed as above until we find a value of x_1 where $|f(x)| < E$.

While finding a value of x where $f(x) = 0$ is clearly our aim, so that testing for $|f(x)| < E$ seems to be reasonable, there may be practical problems involved in implementing this test. This is especially true for functions which change rapidly in the vicinity of the solutions, in which case the accuracy of the computer may not be sufficient to determine a value for x such that $|f(x)| < E$ for a reasonable value of E. We will return to this point shortly.

A much more practical test is to require $|x_1 - x_2| < E_1$ where E_1 is an error limit. When this test is satisfied, x_1 is the solution within an error E_1. For example, if $E_1 = 0.01$, the difference between x_1 and the exact solution would be less than 1%.[†]

This method described above, called interval halving, proceeds as indicated in the following flow chart. (Note that if $A*B > 0$, then A and B are both positive or both negative. If $A*B < 0$, A and B have opposite signs.)

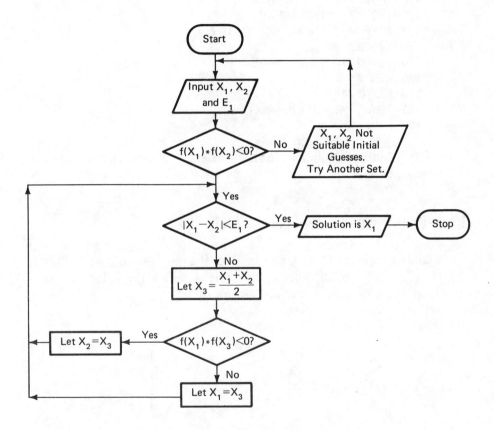

A BASIC Program to implement this procedure is listed below

```
10  PRINT "INTERVAL HALVING ROOTFINDER PROGRAM"
20  REM: THE FUNCTION SHOULD BE PUT IN LINE 40
30  REM: AS THE USER DEFINED FUNCTION FNA(X)
40  DEF FNA(X) = X↑4−24*X↑3−600*X↑2+14400*X−86400.
```

[†] A more sophisticated program might have a combined test. The program proceeds until either $|f(x_1)| < E$ or $|x_1 - x_2| < E_1$ where E and E_1 are error limits.

```
 50  PRINT "INPUT X1, X2, AND E."
 60  INPUT X1, X2, E
 70  IF (FNA(X2)*FNA(X1))<0 THEN 110
 80  PRINT "X1 AND X2 NOT SUITABLE "
 90  PRINT "INPUT NEW VALUES OF X1, X2, AND E."
100  GOTO 60
110  IF ABS(X1−X2)<E THEN 180
120  LET X3=(X1+X2)/2
130  IF (FNA(X3)*FNA(X2))<0 THEN 160
140  LET X2=X3
150  GOTO 110
160  LET X1=X3
170  GOTO 110
180  PRINT "SOLUTION=" X1
190  END
```

The function included in the program is appropriate for the following example.

SAMPLE PROGRAM—Crossing Ladders[†]

Two ladders, one 25 ft long and one 35 ft long, lean against buildings on opposite sides of an alley. The point at which the ladders cross is 12 ft. above the ground. How wide is the alley?

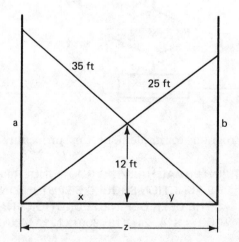

[†]Taken from Gruenberger and Jaffray, *Problems for Computer Solution*, John Wiley.

Using the Pythagorean theorem, we see that

$$z^2 = (35)^2 - a^2 \text{ and}$$
$$z^2 = (25)^2 - b^2$$

so

$$a^2 - b^2 = 600$$

Comparing similar triangles gives us

$$\frac{12}{a} = \frac{y}{z}$$

$$\frac{12}{b} = \frac{x}{z}$$

Since $x + y = z$, we find

$$\frac{12}{a} + \frac{12}{b} = 1.$$

Thus,

$$\frac{12}{b} = 1 - \frac{12}{a}$$

or

$$b = \frac{12a}{a - 12}$$

so

$$a^2 - \left(\frac{12a}{a - 12}\right)^2 = 600$$

or

$$a^4 - 24a^3 - 600a^2 + 14400a - 86400 = 0$$

Once we find a, then

$$z = \sqrt{(35)^2 - a^2}$$

From the geometry we know that a lies between 0 and 35 ft. Using the above program, a = 31.2877 and z = 15.6869.

NUMERICAL INTEGRATION

Many problems which are solved with computers involve numerical integration or finding areas under curves. If, for example, we have the speed of an automobile as a function of time and want the distance traveled in a particular time interval, numerical integration will provide the desired results.

In general, we have some function f(x)

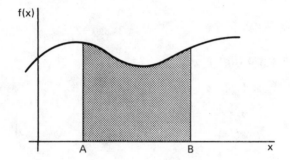

and wish to find the area under the f(x) vrs x curve between A and B. To do this we divide the area into a number (m) of panels by means of m+1 equally spaced parallel lines (including the lines at both ends).

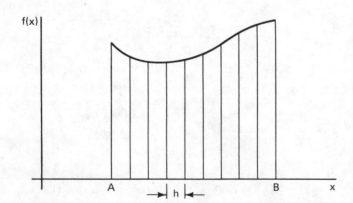

The distance between lines is

$$h = \frac{B - A}{m}$$

To find the approximate area under the curve, consider a single panel. We replace

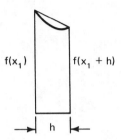

the curve joining the ends of the panel by a straight line. The area of this resulting trapezoid is

$$\text{Area} = \frac{1}{2} h(f(x_1) + f(x_1 + h))$$

Adding the areas of all these little trapezoids together, we get an approximation to the area under the whole curve:

$$\text{Area} = h \left[\frac{1}{2} f(A) + f(A+h) + f(A+2h) + \ldots + f(A+(m-1)h) + \frac{1}{2} f(B) \right]$$

Generally speaking, the larger the number of panels, m, (and, hence, the smaller the panel width, h,) the more accurate the area will be determined. Although this technique is not the most accurate or widely used method, simplicity is its main virtue.

The following program finds the area under (integrates) a function defined in a DEF statement. It can easily be modified to integrate a function provided in the form of discrete data. In this program, A is the initial value of X, B is the final value of X, and m is the number of panels. (In the calculus A and B are called the limits of integration.)

```
 10  PRINT "TRAPEZOIDAL INTEGRATION PROGRAM"
 20  REM:  FUNCTION TO BE INTEGRATED SHOULD APPEAR IN
 30  REM:  LINE 40  AS A USER DEFINED FUNCTION FNA(X)
 40  DEF FNA(X)=SIN(3.14159*X)
 50  PRINT "INPUT INITIAL X, FINAL X, AND NO. OF PANELS"
 60  INPUT X1, X2, M
 70  LET H=(X2—X1)/M
 80  LET S= .5*(FNA(X1)+FNA(X2))
 90  FOR I=1 TO M—1
100  LET S=S+FNA(X1+I*H)
110  NEXT I
120  LET S=S*H
130  PRINT "AREA=";S
140  END
```

SAMPLE PROGRAM

As an example, we calculate the area under the curve $f(x) = SIN(\pi*x)$ for x between 0 and 1. The exact result is area $= 2/\pi = 0.636620$. The following table illustrates how increasing the number of panels increases the accuracy of the calculation.

Number of Panels	Area
10	0.631376
100	0.636568
1000	0.636619
10000	0.636620

As discussed in Chapter 6, increasing the number of panels increases the accuracy only until the effects of round-off errors become important.

LEAST SQUARES DATA FITTING

Every type of experimental measurement involves errors which must be accounted for when interpreting the data. For example, the number of bacteria in a culture increases approximately in an exponential manner in time. Thus,

$$P = P_0 e^{at}$$

where P is the current population, P_0 is the initial population (i.e., the population at t = 0), a is the growth rate and t is the time. Hence e is the base of the natural logarithm.

The population of the culture is estimated at various times by counting the bacteria in a small section of the culture. On the basis of this count, the population of the whole culture is estimated. Since this represents only an estimate of the population, we cannot simply put this population and time into the above relation and solve for the growth rate. Each set of data would provide a different value for a. In fact, P_0 is usually only an estimate. This also adds more uncertainty to any estimate of a.

To obtain a good estimate of a (and P_0) we first take the (natural) logarithm of both sides of this equation, to give

$$\log P = at + \log P_0.$$

Note that log P is a linear function of time. (This is the basis for the fact that an exponential curve becomes a straight line when plotted on "semi-log" graph paper.)

The problem now becomes one of finding values of a and P_0 which "best" fit the data. There are many interesting and important problems which can be put into the form of choosing a linear function of time (or distance or any other independent variable) which "best" fits the data.

The problem can be stated in general terms in the following way: given values of a function f at N different time t_1, t_2, . . ., t_N (we call the values of f at these times $f(t_1)$, $f(t_2)$, . . ., $f(t_N)$), find values of a and b such that

$$at + b$$

"best" represents f(t) for all values of t.

In order to decide what we mean by "best" fit, let $R(t_i)$ (where i is any value between 1 and N) be defined as

$$R(t_i) = f(t_i) - (at_i + b)$$

$R(t_i)$ is called the residue at time t_i. We say a and b are the "best" values when

$$E = \sum_{i=1}^{N} R^2(t_i) = R^2(t_1) + R^2(t_2) + \ldots + R^2(t_N) \text{ is a minimum.}$$

That is, any other values of a and b would produce a larger value of E.

Although the mathematics of finding a and b are somewhat beyond the level of this book, the results are quite simple. Let

$$M1 = \sum_{i=1}^{N} t_i = t_1 + t_2 + \ldots + t_N$$

$$M2 = \sum_{i=1}^{N} t_i = t_1{}^2 + t_2{}^2 + \ldots + t_N{}^2$$

$$M3 = \sum_{i=1}^{N} f(t_i) = f(t_1) + f(t_2) + \ldots + f(t_N)$$

$$M4 = \sum_{i=1}^{N} t_i f(t_i) = t_1 f(t_1) + t_2 f(t_2) + \ldots + t_N f(t_N)$$

Then,

$$a = \frac{N*M4 - M3*M1}{N*M2 - M1*M1}, \quad b = \frac{M3 - a*M1}{N} = \frac{M3*M2 - M1*M4}{N*M2 - M1*M1}$$

The following program calculates a and b:

```
 10   PRINT TAB (12), "LINEAR LEAST SQUARES PROGRAM"
 20   REM: DATA MUST BE ENTERED IN DATA
 30   REM: STATEMENTS STARTING IN LINE 1000
 40   REM: IN THE FOLLOWING ORDER N, T1, F(T1),
 50   REM: T2, F(T2), ... TN, F(TN). UP TO 100
 60   REM: DATA POINTS MAY BE ENTERED
 70   DIM T(100), F(100)
 80   READ N
 90   LET M1=M2=M3=M4=0
100   FOR I=1 TO N
105   READ T(I), F(I)
110   LET M1=M1+T(I)
120   LET M2=M2+T(I)*T(I)
```

```
130  LET M3=M3+F(I)
140  LET M4=M4+T(I)*F(I)
150  NEXT I
160  LET A=(N*M4—M3*M1)/(N*M2—M1*M1)
170  LET B=(M3—A*M1)/N
180  PRINT
185  PRINT "BEST FIT VALUES OF A AND B";
190  PRINT "IN THE EXPRESSION A*T+B ARE"
200  PRINT "A=";A, "B=";B
210  PRINT LIN(2), "DATA SUMMARY"
220  PRINT LIN(1), "T", "F(T)", "A*T+B"
230  PRINT
240  FOR I=1 TO N
250  PRINT T(I), F(I), A*T(I)+B
260  NEXT I
1000 DATA 5, 1, 2, 2, 3, 3, 4, 4, 5, 5, 6
9999 END
```

Whenever possible, a program should be tested on data for which the desired results are already known. The data included in the program above corresponds to exact values for

$$f(t) = t + 1$$

Running this program produces the following output:

LINEAR LEAST SQUARES PROGRAM

BEST FIT VALUES OF A AND B IN THE EXPRESSION A*T+B ARE
A= 1   B= 1

DATA SUMMARY

T	F(T)	A*T+B
1	2	2
2	3	3
3	4	4
4	5	5
5	6	6

DONE

SAMPLE PROGRAM

The following data was taken over a twenty-four hour period for a particular bacterial colony:

Time (hours)	Number of bacteria (millions)	log P
0	1.1	13.91
6	1.7	14.35
12	3.25	14.99
18	5.8	15.57
24	10.2	16.14

Running the above program with this data produces the following output:

LINEAR LEAST SQUARES PROGRAM

BEST FIT VALUES OF A AND B IN THE EXPRESSION A*T+B ARE
A= 9.4669E–02   B= 13.856

DATA SUMMARY

T	F(T)	A*T+B
0	13.91	13.856
6	14.35	14.424
12	14.99	14.992
18	15.57	15.56
24	16.14	16.128

DONE

Here B corresponds to the log P_0, where P_0 is the initial population. The best fit value for P_0 is 1.04 million. Thus, the best fit exponential curve for the population data is

$$P = 1.04 \times 10^6 *EXP(0.09467*T)$$

The least squares method is far more powerful and general than the linear example presented here. Least squares techniques can be used to fit a general polynomial (or any other type of curve) to given data.

PLOTTING ON THE TERMINAL

It is often useful to generate simple plots of data or functions on the terminal. Because of the nature of the terminal, these plots are never very quantitative; but they can be useful in a qualitative way.

Suppose we want to plot a function of the form

$$y = f(x)$$

for x between x_1 and x_2. Assume that the values of y range between y_1 and y_2 and that we divide this range in 50 intervals of width $y_3 = (y_2 - y_1)/50$. On the terminal, the left-most position will correspond to y_1 and the right-most print position to y_2. The intervening positions will correspond to the values $y_1 + y_3$, $y_1 + 2y_3$, . . ., $y_1 + 49y_3$. At each value of x_3 a corresponding value of y will be determined. To plot this function an asterisk (*) will be placed at the print position most nearly corresponding to this value of y. The following program generates labels and axes, and plots the desired functions.

```
10  REM: PLOTTING PROGRAM
20  DEF FNA (X)=SIN(X)
30  PRINT "ENTER XMIN AND XMAX";
40  INPUT X1, X2
50  PRINT "ENTER YMIN AND YMAX";
60  INPUT Y1, Y2
70  PRINT "ENTER NUMBER OF POINTS FOR X";
80  INPUT N1
90  REM: Y3=STEP SIZE FOR Y; X3=STEP SIZE FOR X
100  LET Y3=(Y2-Y1)/50
110  LET X3=(X2-X1)/(N1 - 1)
120  PRINT LIN(3), "LEFT END OF Y AXIS=  "; Y1
130  PRINT "RIGHT END OF Y AXIS=  "; Y2
140  PRINT "INTERVAL FOR Y=  "; Y3
150  PRINT "TOP OF X AXIS=  "; X1
160  PRINT "BOTTOM OF X AXIS=  "; X2
170  PRINT "STEP SIZE IN X=  "; X3
180  PRINT LIN(3)
190  FOR I=1 TO 10
200  PRINT "+ .... ";
210  NEXT I
220  PRINT "+", LIN(0);
```

```
230  FOR I=1 TO N1
240  LET I1=I−1
250  LET N=INT((FNA(I1*X3+X1)−Y1/Y3+.5)
260  IF I1=(5*INT(I1/5)) THEN 290
270  PRINT "."; LIN(0), TAB(N), "*"
280  GOTO 300
290  PRINT "+"; LIN(0), TAB(N), "*"
300  NEXT I
310  END
```

Running the program with the SIN(X) function produces output that looks like

```
ENTER XMIN AND XMAX?0,6.28
ENTER YMIN AND YMAX?−1, 1
ENTER NUMBER OF POINTS FOR X? 21

LEFT END OF Y AXIS=−1
RIGHT END OF Y AXIS= 1
INTERVAL FOR Y= .04
TOP OF X AXIS= 0
BOTTOM OF X AXIS= 6.28
STEP SIZE IN X= .314
```

```
+ . . . . + . . . . + . . . . + . . . . + . . . . * . . . . + . . . . + . . . . + . . . . + . . . . +
.                                                      *
.                                                          *
.                                                              *
.                                                                *
+                                                                  *
.                                                               *
.                                                             *
.                                                          *
.                                                       *
.                                                     *
.                                             *
+                                        *
.                                   *
.                             *
.                        *
.                   *
*              
.            *
.        *
.      *
+    *
```

EXERCISES

1. Joe College is rolling north on Friday evening. He keeps his speed constant for five minute intervals starting at 15 miles per hour leaving Charlottesville. Being anxious to arrive promptly, he increases his speed (essentially instantaneously) by 10% for each successive interval. Write a computer program in BASIC that will compute and print out the time required for him to get to Madison, Virginia (40 miles from Charlottesville). The program should also print out the speed at the time of arrival in Madison and the average speed for the trip.

2. A car weighing 1000 kg contains an engine which produces a propulsive force F which is inversely proportional to the speed of the car (at high speeds) given by

$$F = 60000/V$$

with F in newtons when V is in meters per second. The aerodynamic resistance D is given by $D = .05V^2$, with D in newtons when V is in meters per second. The resistance due to rolling friction is a constant force of 100 newtons. Write a computer program in BASIC that will compute (and print out) the maximum speed attainable by the car to the closest 1 meter/sec.

    HINT: The maximum velocity occurs when the net force on the car is zero.

3. Write a program in BASIC which will solve the equation $x = \exp(-x)$ to provide a value of x correct to four decimal places.

4. Mr. Rock Zinhead inadvertently entered I-64 to Richmond before it was opened. Not being very bright, he mistook the signs giving the distance to Richmond for the speed limit signs. Since Mr. Zinhead was very law abiding, he always traveled at the posted speed limits. Write a program in BASIC that will compute and print out the time required for him to reach Richmond. (Note: distance traveled = speed * time) Assume that he began his trip 65 miles from Richmond and that the distance signs were placed at the entrance ramp and were located every 5 miles. Assume further that he was able to slow down to the desired speed essentially instantaneously. The program should also compute and print out the average speed for the trip.

5. The flight speed-dependence of the aerodynamic resistance of a Boeing 737 aircraft is given by the expression

$$D(V) = A/V^2 + BV^2 + C \exp(V/K)$$

with D given in pounds force when V is in miles per hour and the drag parameters are:

$$A = 2.42 \times 10^8 \, \text{lb} \cdot (\text{mph})^2, \quad B = 0.07 \, \text{lb}/(\text{mph})^2,$$
$$C = 1.66 \, \text{lb}, \quad K = 70 \, \text{mph}$$

This aircraft contains two Pratt and Whitney JT-8D turbofan engines, each of which can provide up to 12500 pounds of thrust (independent of flight speed). Write a program in BASIC that will compute (and print out) the minimum flight speed of this aircraft to the closest 1 mile per hour. (HINT: The minimum velocity occurs when the drag force equals the thrust.)

6. Write a program to plot $f(x) = 1/(1 + x^2)$ for x between 0 and 2.

7. From problem 5 above, write a program to plot the aerodynamic resistance, D, of a Boeing 737 aircraft as a function of speed, V.

9

Other Features in BASIC

The material presented in Chapters 2 through 7 is common among most versions of BASIC. Programs written using this material should run almost anywhere with little or no modification. There are, however, several other features in BASIC which are very common but not standard. While their characteristics are similar, their implementation varies greatly from version to version. The basic concepts are given here. However, the reader is referred to the user manual for specific details. The topics to be covered in this chapter include string variables, print-using and files.

STRING VARIABLES

In Chapter 5, we discussed strings in relation to the PRINT statement. Strings, you will recall, consist of a set of characters (except quotation marks) enclosed in quotation marks. For example:

> "GOOD-BY"
> "TIME OUT"
> "123597"
> "@??"

are all strings. Note that numbers can be written as strings by enclosing them in quotation marks. However, when a number is enclosed in quotation marks, it is treated as a string and as such cannot be added, subtracted, multiplied or divided. It is treated like any other set of characters—not like a number.

Most BASIC versions have string variables which are defined as a letter[†] followed by a dollar sign. Eg.

A$, B$, R$.

The number of characters that can be stored in a string variable varies from version to version. In some cases the allowed length of the string can be changed by including it in a DIM statement. Using a DIM statement, the length of a string (i.e. number of characters allowed) can usually be increased to 64 or more characters. In some versions the length of strings are fixed.

Most versions allow singly subscripted string variables such as A$(5), Z$(7), etc. When permitted, the subscripted string variable should appear in a DIM statement just as subscripted numeric variables do.

For our discussion, we will assume that any string variable we use can have up to 15 characters. This restriction, however, does not affect the general ideas.

Strings can appear in READ statements. For example,

10 READ A$

Strings and numeric data can be mixed in a READ statement. For example,

20 READ A$, B, C1, Z9, Z$

The data in the DATA statement must be of the corresponding type. When the READ statement calls for a string variable, the next item in the DATA list must be a string variable. When a numeric variable is required, a number (not in quotations) must be next in the data list.

When a string appears in a data statement, it must be enclosed in quotation marks. A DATA statement appropriate for line 20 above might be

100 DATA "TIME", 3.6, 7.528, 3.14159, "OUT"

String variables can be assigned with LET statements.

[†] Some versions allow a letter and a digit followed by a $; e.g., A3$, C9$, Z∅$.

```
30  LET B$ = "YES"
40  LET RS = "NO"
```

String variables can be assigned with an INPUT statement. Thus

```
50  INPUT A$
```

is legitimate. When a single string variable appears in an input statement, the response to the question mark need not be put in quotation
marks. An appropriate response to

```
50  INPUT A$
```

would be

```
?  YES
```

If several string variables or string variables and numeric variables
appear in an input statement, the string variable information must be
in quotation marks. If

```
60  INPUT A$, ZØ, B$
```

is executed, a suitable response would be

```
?  "YES", 3.8, "NO"
```

An important use of string variables in INPUT statements is
in "conversational programming". The following program segment
illustrates how useful this can be.

```
100  PRINT "DO YOU WISH TO CONTINUE";
110  INPUT A$
120  IF A$ = "YES" THEN 140
130  GO TO 500
140  REM CONTINUE WITH PROGRAM
     .
     .
     .
500  END
```

This example also illustrates that string variables can be compared
in an IF . . . THEN statement.

All six types of comparisons discussed in Chapter 2 can be performed with string variables.

Two strings are equal when they are identical. When comparing two strings, blanks and punctuation are important.

Thus if A$ = "GOOD-BY" and B$ = "GOODBY" then A$ is not equal to B$. If A$ is changed to

A$ = "GOOD BY"

A$ and B$ are still not equal.

Leading and trailing blanks are counted in these comparisons. Changing A$ to A$ = "GOODBY " leaves A$ and B$ unequal. (Note that when using an input statement with a single string, leading and trailing blanks are not included as part of the string unless the entire string is enclosed in quotation marks.)

When strings consist of alphabetic characters, a string is less than another string when it would appear in an alphabetic list before the second string.

If A$ = "GOODBY" and B$ = "ACORN" then B$ is less than A$. This comparison process is performed just as if you were alphabetizing a list. Starting with the left most character, working to the right, characters are compared until a difference is encountered or one string runs out of characters. For example

A$ = "GOOD"
B$ = "GOODBY"

then A$ is less than B$.

For characters other than the letters of the alphabet, the actual ordering varies from version to version. The user's manual has a list of all characters and their order.

PRINTUSING

In Chapter 5, we discussed printing and saw that the computer can print numbers out in several formats depending on the size of the number and the number of significant digits.

When producing tables or reports, it is usually desirable to have all numbers printed in the same format. This is especially true when the numbers represent dollar amounts.

PRINTUSING allows the user to specify exactly the form for printing. The actual way the format is specified varies greatly among the versions of BASIC so will not be covered here.

There are, however, some general features that you should be aware of. For printing numbers, the PRINTUSING statement allows the user to specify the number of digits to the right of the decimal and to the left. Thus when printing dollar amounts, generally two digits are printed to the right of the decimal. Rounding is done automatically— when a number is printed using PRINTUSING, the number is rounded to the specified number of decimal places. Dollar signs and commas can be placed in appropriate places. The decimal point is always printed in the same column so that tables of dollar amounts (or any other kind of numbers) are printed in columns.

PRINTUSING can also be used to print strings and combinations of strings and numbers in nicely layed-out columns.

FILES

We have already seen that it is possible to store data in the computer for use by a particular program by using DATA statements. Often, however, it is desirable to store the data independent of a particular program, especially when the data is needed by several different programs. Most versions of BASIC allow you to store data in "Data files".

Unfortunately, each version of BASIC handles files somewhat differently, so we will have to be content with pointing out some of the principal features and uses of files.

Generally speaking, a file is a reserved area on the mass storage device. Files are much more powerful than DATA statements since a program can both read from and write into files. In fact, a given program can access several files at one time.

Once a file is written, it remains available for use—either to be read or rewritten until the user decides that it is no longer needed. Thus if you write a file today, it will remain[†] on the mass storage device until you need it again next week.

[†] Some large systems periodically remove inactive files to make space available to other users. Be sure to check the policy on your system if you plan to leave a file unused for an extended period of time.

10

Projects

PROJECT 1 SIMULATION OF A SELF-REPRODUCING SYSTEM

The purpose of this project is to simulate the growth of a colony of self-reproducing organisms under conditions of limited food supply. The result to be obtained (and depicted graphically) is the time-dependence of the population of the colony.

We start the simulation by defining a field or area to which the colony of organisms is confined and in which it can grow. Suppose we represent the field by an 11 × 11 array of numbers. Any non-zero element of the array represents an organism; the value of the element represents the size of the organism. We start by placing one organism of size 10 in the middle of our array, at location (6, 6). The initial organism array then looks like this:

```
0   0   0   0   0   0    0   0   0   0   0
0   0   0   0   0   0    0   0   0   0   0
0   0   0   0   0   0    0   0   0   0   0
0   0   0   0   0   0    0   0   0   0   0
0   0   0   0   0   0    0   0   0   0   0
0   0   0   0   0   10   0   0   0   0   0
0   0   0   0   0   0    0   0   0   0   0
0   0   0   0   0   0    0   0   0   0   0
0   0   0   0   0   0    0   0   0   0   0
0   0   0   0   0   0    0   0   0   0   0
0   0   0   0   0   0    0   0   0   0   0
```

We want to simulate growth by the mechanism of an organism eating food. Let us imagine a food array, of the same size as the organism array, which represents the food available to an organism at each point of the array. The initial food array then looks like this:

5	5	5	5	5	5	5	5	5	5	5
5	5	5	5	5	5	5	5	5	5	5
5	5	5	5	5	5	5	5	5	5	5
5	5	5	5	5	5	5	5	5	5	5
5	5	5	5	5	5	5	5	5	5	5
5	5	5	5	5	0	5	5	5	5	5
5	5	5	5	5	5	5	5	5	5	5
5	5	5	5	5	5	5	5	5	5	5
5	5	5	5	5	5	5	5	5	5	5
5	5	5	5	5	5	5	5	5	5	5
5	5	5	5	5	5	5	5	5	5	5

We next need to agree on some general rules to simulate the processes of eating food, growing, and self-reproduction. When an organism moves to a new location, if there is food at this location, it eats the food and grows in size by adding the value of the food array element to its own value. Thus, if an organism of size 10 moves to a location with food value 5, the size of the organism becomes 15. Of course, since the food has been eaten, the food value is now 0.

We shall restrict an organism's moves to the horizontal and vertical directions and allow it to move one space at a time. There are thus 4 directions it can move and we shall use a random process to select the direction it does move. We shall have to give special consideration to an organism that is on the edge of the array because its choice of movement directions is restricted. Only one organism can occupy a space or point in the array. Thus, when an organism is completely surrounded by other organisms, it cannot move until a path opens and so it loses its turn.

Self-reproduction is achieved by an organism subdividing into two organisms when it reaches the size of 20. (Each resulting organism has a new size of 10.) One of the resulting organisms moves on the next turn if a move is possible, the other moves on the following turn. This subdivision is the only method by which the number of organisms grows.

The concept of a "turn" is used to simulate a unit of time in real life. By a turn we mean stepping through the array, allowing each organism that can move to do so and if food is present at the new location, to eat that food. This turn represents one unit of time. However, we must be careful to avoid always stepping through the array in the same manner, e.g. starting at the upper left hand corner. This will introduce an artificial bias. We should randomly change the place at which we start our turn and the direction of stepping.

The question of bias brings us to the question of what checks we can make to see if we are achieving a reasonable simulation. You will note that there is a conservation principle at work since the sum of organism and food values should remain constant. This sum can be checked. Furthermore, we can visually inspect our organism array and note if the distribution of organisms appears to be uniform. For example, we might subdivide the organism array into 4 sub-arrays and count the number of organisms in each sub-array. These counts should be approximately equal for large arrays, but may differ considerably for the small array we are using.

The final result is to be an organism growth curve. This curve is a plot of number of organisms versus time. We represent each unit of time by one turn. To get points for the growth curve, you can run the problem several times, stopping each time after a given number of turns and then counting the number of organisms. An alternate procedure would be to make a single turn, printing out the number of organisms at every unit of time.

One purpose of this project is to give you an open-ended problem and to encourage you to develop your own rules and procedures for a successful simulation. However, you must specify and justify these rules.

A suggested flowchart for the required computer algorithm is attached.

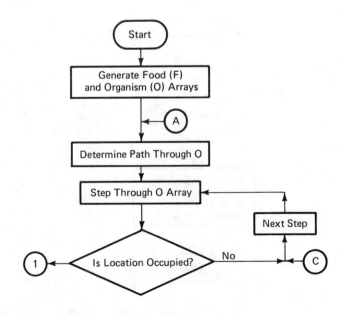

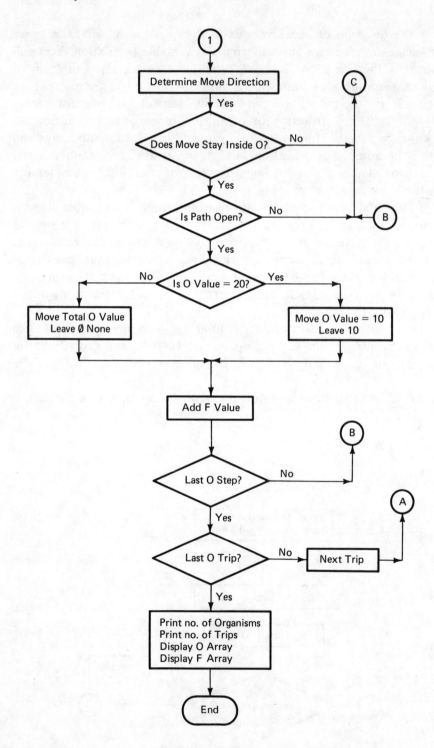

PROJECT 2 COMPUTER GRAPHICS

Computer graphics and computer aided design are fields which have grown very rapidly as a result of computer technology. The applications of computer graphics range from engineering design and analysis to data reduction, and new applications are constantly being discovered.

In general, a computer graphics program consists of the input, the manipulation, and the output of graphical data. This project will consist of the first two, and the output will be missing. If a remote plotter were available at your terminal, the results of this project could be plotted, but in our case, you will be asked to take the values and manually plot them on a sheet of paper.

The manipulation of graphical data is most frequently handled by the use of matrices. Also, matrices are used to store a great deal of graphical information. This project is an application which will illustrate the storage and manipulation of graphical data. Specifically, the application is to refine the information obtained from an aerial photograph. This is an example of two dimensional graphics. Many other applications in computer graphics are three dimensional such as describing the shapes of automobile bodies, structural analysis of buildings, and design of machine parts.

This project is an example of the use of matrices to manipulate graphical information. Specifically, the project illustrates an application involving two dimensional graphical information. The data are coordinates of a set of points (x, y) in a plane. These points are connected to form the shape of a piece of property.

The project involves an aerial photograph of this piece of property. The photograph is known to be distorted, and the object of the project is to obtain a correct, undistorted view of the property.

A drawing or picture can be thought of as a set of (x, y) points and can be represented by a matrix. If the drawing has n points the matrix would be:

$$\begin{bmatrix} x_1 & x_2 & x_3 & \cdots & x_n \\ y_1 & y_2 & y_3 & \cdots & y_n \end{bmatrix} = P$$

If such a matrix is multiplied by a 2×2 matrix (M) the result will produce a new (2×n) Matrix (N)

$$\begin{bmatrix} a & b \\ c & d \end{bmatrix} \begin{bmatrix} x_1 & x_2 & x_3 & \cdots & x_n \\ y_1 & y_2 & y_3 & \cdots & y_n \end{bmatrix} = \begin{bmatrix} x_1' & x_2' & x_3' & \cdots & x_n' \\ y_1' & y_2' & y_3' & \cdots & y_n' \end{bmatrix}$$

$$\text{M} \qquad\qquad\qquad \text{P} \qquad\qquad\qquad\qquad \text{N}$$

The exception would be if matrix M were an identity matrix

$$\begin{bmatrix} 1 & 0 \\ 0 & 1 \end{bmatrix}$$

in which case no change would take place and matrix P and N would be identical. An example of this is the drawing shown in Figure 1. The five points and their coordinates are:

Point	1	2	3	4	5
X	1	1	1	3	2
Y	1	2	3	3	2

$$F = \begin{bmatrix} 1 & 1 & 1 & 3 & 2 \\ 1 & 2 & 3 & 3 & 2 \end{bmatrix}$$

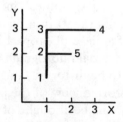

Figure 1

Some examples of matrices typically used are:

1. Rotation

$$\begin{bmatrix} c & s \\ -s & c \end{bmatrix} \begin{bmatrix} x \\ y \end{bmatrix} = \begin{bmatrix} x^1 \\ y^1 \end{bmatrix}$$

rotation clockwise about origin $\Theta°$, where c = cos Θ and s = sin Θ. If s = −sin Θ, rotation is counter clockwise.

An example of a rotation is shown in Figure 2. This letter F is rotated 30° clockwise.

R*F = G

cosine 30° = .866

sine 30° = .50

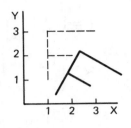

Figure 2

$$\begin{bmatrix} .866 & .5 \\ -.5 & .866 \end{bmatrix} \begin{bmatrix} 1 & 1 & 1 & 3 & 2 \\ 1 & 2 & 3 & 3 & 2 \end{bmatrix} = \begin{bmatrix} 1.37 & 1.87 & 2.37 & 4.10 & 2.73 \\ .37 & 1.23 & 2.10 & 1.10 & .73 \end{bmatrix}$$

$$\qquad\ R \qquad\qquad\quad F \qquad\qquad\qquad\qquad G$$

2. Stretch/Shrink

$$\begin{bmatrix} j & 0 \\ 0 & k \end{bmatrix} \begin{bmatrix} x \\ y \end{bmatrix} = \begin{bmatrix} x' \\ y' \end{bmatrix}$$

stretch/shrink: if $j = k = 2$, picture would double in size in the x and y directions. If $j = k = .5$, picture would reduce to half size. If $j = 3$ and $k = .1$, picture would expand in the x and shrink in the y direction.

An example of this is shown in Figure 3.

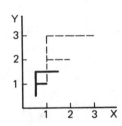

Figure 3

$$\begin{bmatrix} .5 & 0 \\ 0 & .5 \end{bmatrix} \begin{bmatrix} 1 & 1 & 1 & 3 & 2 \\ 1 & 2 & 3 & 3 & 2 \end{bmatrix} = \begin{bmatrix} .5 & .5 & .5 & 1.5 & 1 \\ .5 & 1 & 1.5 & 1.5 & 1 \end{bmatrix}$$

$$\qquad\ S \qquad\qquad\quad F \qquad\qquad\qquad\qquad H$$

3. **Reflection (see 2.)** If $j = -1$, $k = 1$, picture is reflected about the y axis to produce its mirror image. If $(j = 1, k = -1)$, picture is reflected about x axis.

$$P = \begin{bmatrix} -1 & 0 \\ 0 & 1 \end{bmatrix}$$

$$Q = \begin{bmatrix} 1 & 0 \\ 0 & -1 \end{bmatrix}$$

$$P*Q = \begin{bmatrix} -1 & 0 \\ 0 & -1 \end{bmatrix}$$

$$P*F = J$$

$$Q*F = L$$

$$P*Q*F = K$$

See Figure 4 for the results of these multiplications.

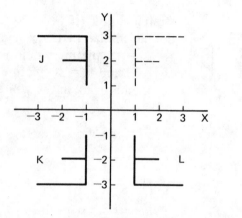

Figure 4

$$\begin{bmatrix} -1 & 0 \\ 0 & 1 \end{bmatrix} \begin{bmatrix} 1 & 1 & 1 & 3 & 2 \\ 1 & 2 & 3 & 3 & 2 \end{bmatrix} = \begin{bmatrix} -1 & -1 & -1 & -3 & -2 \\ 1 & 2 & 3 & 3 & 2 \end{bmatrix}$$

$$\quad\quad P \quad\quad\quad\quad\quad F \quad\quad\quad\quad\quad\quad\quad\quad J$$

4. **Shear** $\begin{bmatrix} 1 & m \\ n & 1 \end{bmatrix}$ If either m or n are not zero, a shearing takes place.

For example $\begin{bmatrix} 1 & 1 \\ 0 & 1 \end{bmatrix}$ would put vertical lines at 45°.

An example of this is shown in Figure 5.

$$Z = \begin{bmatrix} 1 & .7 \\ 0 & 1 \end{bmatrix}$$

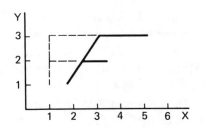

Figure 5

$Z*F = M$

$$\begin{bmatrix} 1 & .7 \\ 0 & 1 \end{bmatrix} \begin{bmatrix} 1 & 1 & 1 & 3 & 2 \\ 1 & 2 & 3 & 3 & 2 \end{bmatrix} = \begin{bmatrix} 1.7 & 2.4 & 3.1 & 5.1 & 3.4 \\ 1 & 2 & 3 & 3 & 2 \end{bmatrix}$$
$\quad\quad$ Z $\quad\quad\quad\quad\quad$ F $\quad\quad\quad\quad\quad\quad\quad$ M

These matrices may be used in combination. For example, use R, S and P from the first three types just discussed and multiply the data F.

$R*S*P*F = N$

$$\begin{bmatrix} .866 & .5 \\ -.5 & .866 \end{bmatrix} \begin{bmatrix} .5 & 0 \\ 0 & .5 \end{bmatrix} \begin{bmatrix} -1 & 0 \\ 0 & 1 \end{bmatrix} \begin{bmatrix} 1 & 1 & 1 & 3 & 2 \\ 1 & 2 & 3 & 3 & 2 \end{bmatrix} =$$

$$\begin{bmatrix} -.433 & .25 \\ .25 & .433 \end{bmatrix} \begin{bmatrix} 1 & 1 & 1 & 3 & 2 \\ 1 & 2 & 3 & 3 & 2 \end{bmatrix} =$$

$$\begin{bmatrix} -.18 & .07 & .32 & -.55 & -.37 \\ .68 & 1.12 & 1.55 & 2.05 & 1.37 \end{bmatrix}$$
$\quad\quad\quad\quad\quad\quad\quad$ N

The result is shown in Figure 6.

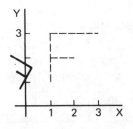

Figure 6

In this project, Figure 7 on page 147 is based on an aerial photograph of a piece of property. Assume the points all lie in the xy plane, and that for some reason the drawing in Figure 7 is distorted. You are furnished enough information about the true property to find the true shape.

If an origin and the coordinates of 2 points are known both before and after undergoing a change, the matrix used to make the change can be found. Let M, N and P be 2X2 matrices. Let P be 2 points from the drawing in Figure 1, M be an unknown matrix and N be the same two points in the new (undistorted) drawing.

$$M * P = N$$
$$M * P * P^{-1} = N * P^{-1}$$
$$M = N * P^{-1}$$

After you have solved for matrix M, use it to compute new coordinates for all 13 points. Sketch in the true shape on the gridded paper to a scale of $1'' = 40'$.

After the corrected coordinates have been found, write a program to compute the area of the property. One method for computing the area is to break up the area into vertical strips, each strip being a trapezoid with area $= .5 * \Delta x * (y1 + y2)$.

The data for the shape shown in Figure 7 are:

Point	1	2	3	4	5	6	7	8	9	10	11	12	13
x	−100	−100	80	160	20	10	0	−8	−9	−7	0	20	70
y	−100	100	140	60	30	28.5	22.5	10	0	−10	−21.5	−40	−90

Also, it is known that the correct coordinates for two points in the undistorted shape are:

Point	1	4
x	−132	200
y	−71	24.5

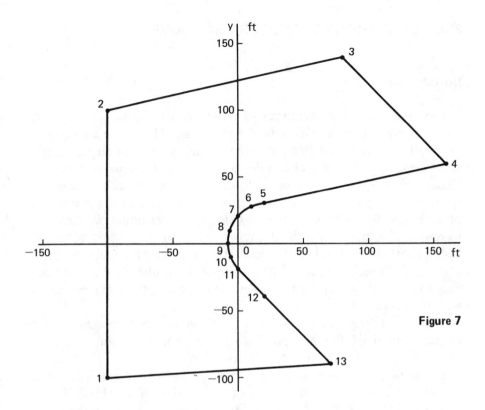

Figure 7

General Discussion:

This method of using matrices to transform data is useful for both two dimensional and three dimensional data.

This project illustrates a possible two dimensional application, that of correcting data obtained from aerial photographs.

In three dimensional space, solid objects may be manipulated by a similar technique of computer programming, using matrices. This type of program allows the engineering designer to move solid objects to various positions in space, to rotate certain portions of data, to change the size and shape of objects, and to always retain a mathematical model of the results throughout the design sequence. The data resulting from the program may be analyzed (for example, we computed an area), it may be drawn for inspection, and in some cases, the data may be output on a tape which can then manufacture the part on a numerically controlled machine.

The majority of engineering design problems involve some graphics, and many graphical programs use matrix multiplication to manipulate the data during the design process.

PROJECT 3   THE GREAT MOTORCYCLE JUMP

Introduction

Simulation is the technique of imitating a real process. For example, one might want to simulate the processing of jobs on a computer, the motion of neutrons in an atomic reactor, the flow of aircraft traffic at an airport, or the arrival of telephone calls at a telephone exchange. Once a working simulation of a physical process has been obtained, it is usually quite easy to alter the various parameters of the model and observe how it operates with these changes. For example, we may wish to change the rate of arrival of aircraft at an airport and/or the landing and takeoff times, or alter the geometry of a uranium fuel element in a reactor. Experimenting with a computer simulation of a physical process is often much faster, easier, and cheaper than experimenting with the process itself.

The first stage in the design of a simulation is to make a mathematical model of the process. Two types of models can be used to describe a process, viz., a deterministic model or a probabilistic model. For example, Newton's laws of classical mechanics are a mathematical model which govern the dynamics of the motion of an object. Such a model is deterministic in that the characteristics of the motion, e.g., the displacement, the velocity, and the acceleration, are determined by equations. However, it is not always possible to make such a model of a real process. Consider the simple operation of flipping a coin. Although Newtonian mechanics should predict whether the coin will land heads or tails (given the initial velocity, spin, height, etc.) in practice it is impossible to determine this in advance. Consequently, a deterministic model cannot be used. Instead, we can make a probabilistic model of this process by noting that the probability that the coin lands heads equals one half. Although such models will not determine precisely what will happen, a great deal can be learned about the physical process by studying such models of, e.g., the flow of aircraft through an air traffic control zone, or the diffusion of neutrons through the wall of a reactor.

Given a model of either type, it often happens that the mathematical formulation is difficult or even impossible to solve in practice. However, it is possible to obtain approximate solutions to the problem by simulating the physical process with the computer, and simulation is a very powerful method of obtaining approximate solutions to otherwise intractable problems.

Motion of a Body

As an example of a deterministic simulation, consider the motion of a body under the influence of external forces. This motion is determined by the laws of Newtonian mechanics. In a practical situation, these laws, when expressed as a mathematical model, are usually impossible to solve by standard mathematical techniques. We can, however, simulate the motion of a body, e.g., a rocket, planet, or projectile, on a computer and thus observe how the system performs under differing conditions. Consider first the simple situation of an object of mass M, initially at rest, acted on by a force F. The force produces an acceleration A, and the mathematical model of the system is given by $F = M * A$ or $A = F/M$. The acceleration produced by the force can be used to determine the velocity and distance travelled at any given time. (This problem can be solved easily using standard mathematical techniques.) To simulate the motion, we consider small time intervals of length I. Assume that the simulation has proceeded for several time intervals and that at time T the velocity is V and the distance travelled is S. We wish to evaluate the new velocity and new distance at the end of the next time interval (T + I). Since the acceleration is the rate of change of velocity, the velocity at time (T + I) is given by

$$V \leftarrow V + A * I \tag{1}$$

Similarly, since the velocity is the rate of change of displacement, the distance travelled at time (T + I) is given by

$$S \leftarrow S + V * I \tag{2}$$

The velocity used in Equation (2) may be either the velocity at time T or the velocity at time (T + I). In practice, the time interval is chosen sufficiently small such that the difference is negligible, and we shall adopt the convention that the velocity is always altered before the distance. Essentially, we have discretized a continuous process, which means that our simulation model is only an approximation to the actual process. The smaller we choose I, the better our approximation will be (subject, of course, to the restriction that the rounding errors introduced by computing so many quantities do not combine to cause a decrease in the overall accuracy of the method).

Consider now the problem faced by a publicity-seeking stuntman who is considering "jumping" across a large canyon on a vehicle that can best be described as a modified motorcycle. The general plan is to provide a flat acceleration area whose maximum length, Z, is specified. The vehicle, whose mass is M, is equipped with a propulsive device, e.g., a jet engine, that delivers a constant thrust, F. A takeoff ramp having an elevation angle E is located at the end of the runway. The width of the canyon is W, and the landing area is located at a vertical distance H above the acceleration area. The flat landing area has a maximum length L.

To simulate the motion of the vehicle, we first made a deterministic model of the process. For convenience, designate the horizontal components of position, velocity, and acceleration as X, V1, and A1, respectively, and the corresponding vertical components by Y, V2, and A2. The vehicle is assumed to accelerate from rest along the runway under the influence of the (constant) propulsive thrust F and the aerodynamic resistance D. At the end of the runway, the ramp imparts a vertical velocity component to the vehicle such that the flight path is inclined at an (initial) angle E to the horizontal. While airborne, the vehicle is influenced by its weight (M * G) and by the aerodynamic resistance D. The vehicle is required to land within the specified landing area with a vertical component of impact velocity below a critical value V3. Since the equations of motion are difficult to solve in practice, the motion can be simulated by considering small time intervals of length I. After selecting a time step I, the changes in the components of acceleration, velocity, and position can be calculated from Newton's 2nd Law of Motion in the following manner:

1. Motion on the Runway

The runway motion is purely horizontal. Neglecting ground friction, the only forces to be considered are the propulsive thrust F and the aerodynamic drag D. The drag can be expressed as

$$D = K * V * V$$

where

$$K = \text{drag coefficient (constant)}$$
$$V = \text{SQR } (V1 * V1 + V2 * V2)$$
$$= \text{resultant velocity}$$

then

$$A1 = (F-D)/M, \qquad\qquad A2 = 0$$
$$V1 = V1 + ((F-K*V*V)/M)* I, \qquad V2 = 0$$

2. Motion on the Ramp

When the vehicle reaches the takeoff ramp, the direction (but not the magnitude) of the resultant velocity is assumed to change instantaneously. Hence,

$$V1 = V1 * (\text{COS } (E))$$
$$V2 = V1 * (\text{SIN } (E))$$

(This implies that the time spent on the ramp is negligible when compared to the total flight time.)

3. Motion in Flight

After leaving the ramp the engine is cut off, and the vehicle follows a trajectory under the influence of gravitational and drag forces. Thus,

$$A1 = -D*\text{COS}(A)/M$$
$$A2 = -D*\text{SIN}(A)/M-G$$
$$V1 = V1 - (K*V*V * \text{COS } (A)/M)*I$$
$$V2 = V2 - (K*V*V*\text{SIN}(A)/M+G)*I$$

where

$$A = \text{ATN } (V2/V1)$$

A flow chart of the simulation is given in Figure 1.

Problem

Consider a vehicle whose total mass is 500 kg including the propulsion system which produces a constant thrust of 10,000 newtons. The gravitational acceleration is 9.8m/sec^2, and the drag coefficient can be taken as 1/25. The maximum vertical component of impact velocity is 10m/sec. Take Z = 2000m, W = 1200m, L = 100m, and H = 100m.

1. Write a computer program to simulate the motion of the vehicle. The program should accept the starting distance from the ramp and the ramp angle as input, and then determine the vehicle trajectory. Plot a graph of trajectory (either by hand or a computer plot).

2. Experiment with various starting distances and ramp angles until a trajectory meeting all of the constraints is obtained. Estimate the influence of the time interval I and the drag coefficient K on the results.

3. There are many additional factors which can be explored including:

   (a) maximum altitude and time to reach maximum altitude.

   (b) effect of the elevation of the opposite canyon wall relative to the runway.

   (c) other possible trajectory conditions (in principle, a ramp angle-starting distance map could be produced giving the results of all possible combinations).

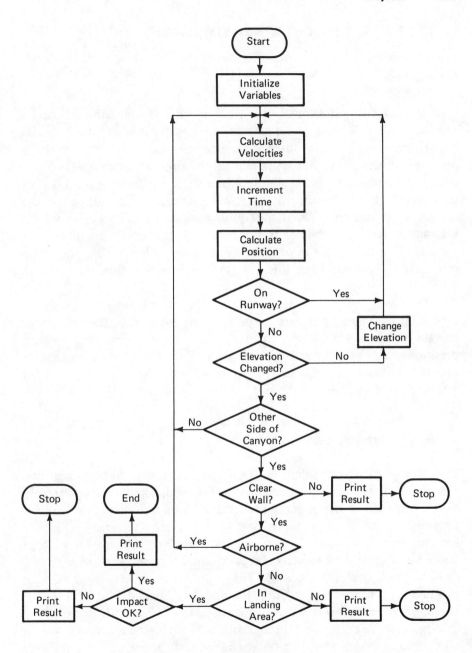

Figure 1

PROJECT 4   THE SUPERTANKER SIMULATOR

Introduction

One of the important uses of a computer is simulating processes where precise mathematical equations to describe the situation cannot be written down because there is an element of chance or uncertainty in some of the relevant parameters of the problem. Examples of this process, called probabilistic simulation, include the landing and take-off of aircraft at an airport, the traffic patterns in large cities, or the motion (position and velocity) of molecules in a gas. In such problems we cannot say for certain that a particular event will occur; at best we can assign or estimate the probability of an event happening. Nevertheless, many problems have this character and must still be analyzed to obtain useful results.

One way of modeling such processes is to assign appropriate probabilities based upon past experience or theoretical considerations and then to replicate the process many times using a computer. We then presume that the average of many such trials should be a reasonable estimate of how the process will behave. This technique is often called a Monte Carlo method.

Problem — Refinery Berth Expansion

This particular problem is based upon an actual problem that was solved for an Esso (Exxon) refinery in England. The refinery currently has 5 berths where ocean-going tankers can dock to unload crude oil for the refinery to process. Only <u>one</u> of the berths is large enough to accommodate the large "super tankers" of 150,000 tons. These large tankers are scheduled to arrive on every <u>third</u> day and they require <u>two</u> days to dock, unload and exit. The problem is to decide whether it would be economically justified to modify a second berth so that it could also accommodate the super tankers. The modifications, including amortization of capital costs and maintenance costs, would cost $200,000 annually. If a tanker has to wait, it will cost the refinery $5,000 per day of waiting.

Although tankers are scheduled to arrive every three days, they may be early or late due to weather, dock strikes, etc., so that their actual arrival day is uncertain. Based upon past experiences, the following probabilities for arrivals can be estimated.

Arrival	Probability
on time	30%
1 day late	20%
1 day early	10%
2 days late	10%
2 days early	10%
3 days late	10%
4 days late	10%

Assignment

1. Make use of the attached flow chart to write a program that will simulate, over a year's period, the arrival, waiting and docking of supertankers at the refinery along with their associated costs. Note that it is necessary to simulate two cases: only one berth large enough and two berths large enough. The flow chart on page 156 is written for the single berth case and must be modified for two large berths. The program should provide for running the simulation a number of times (20, 40 etc.) until the average yearly cost becomes independent of the number of simulations run.

   Run your program to determine whether it is economically justified to modify a second berth for super tankers. Include in your print-out the arrival times of the ships for one of your simulations. Print out and plot the average yearly costs for one and two berths as a function of the number of simulations.

2. Discuss your results including answers to such questions as:

   a. At what remodeling cost is the break-even point?

   b. How many simulations do I need to run to get a reliable answer? How sensitive do you think this is to the arrival probabilities?

Extensions

You might like to improve on the simulation by considering additional questions such as:

1. What would be the effect of different arrival probabilities on the economics?

2. If the refinery expanded so that it needed a super tanker every two days, should you modify zero, one or two berths?

3. ? (your ideas).

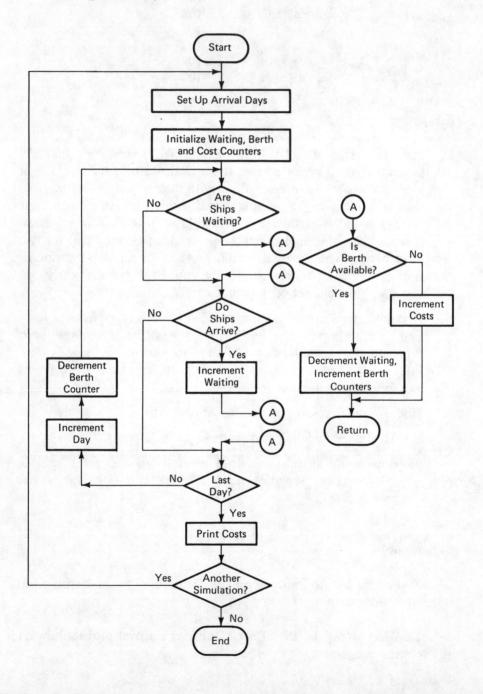

PROJECT 5   THE AREA UNDER A CURVE

Joe Counterspy has bugged the aircraft of an enemy agent by placing on board a small device which transmits the airplane's ground speed. He wants to know the distance that the plane travels before landing. However, since aircraft are not equipped with odometers, he has to settle for the ground speed. Joe has come to us for help, bringing with him a time record of the ground speed that looks like this:

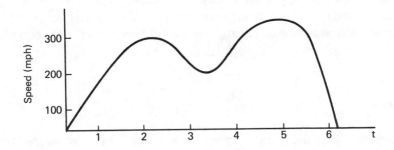

If the ground speed were constant, we could help him very easily since, for a constant speed, S, the distance, D, traveled in a time, T, is simply

$$D = S * T$$

However, we see from the speed-time record that the speed is not constant but is a rather complicated function of time. Since Joe persists in wanting an answer, we must do something to help him.

One approach to the problem is to divide the flight time into a number of short intervals of length I and approximate the speed during each interval by a constant. This is shown schematically below.

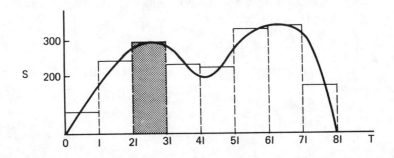

Here we have divided the total flight time into 8 intervals (of length 3/4 hours). In each interval, we selected the speed in the middle of the interval for our constant value. The distance traveled in a given time interval with the constant speed is simply the area of the rectangle as indicated for the third interval. (Note that the height of the rectangle is just the (constant) speed and the width of the rectangle is the time interval I.)

In order to find the total distance traveled, we simply sum the areas of all of the rectangles. Since the actual distance traveled is the area under the curve, the area under the rectangles is only an approximation. However, if we determine the distance traveled to within a mile, Joe will be satisfied. Clearly, as we take more and more (smaller) intervals, the accuracy of our approximation becomes better and better.

Problem

Assume that the ground speed, S, is given by the following function of time, T:

$$S = T*(6-T)*(50-4*T*(6-T)) \qquad 0 \leqslant T \leqslant 6$$

with S in mph and T in hours.

A. Draw a flowchart illustrating the logic of a computer program which performs the following tasks:

1) Calculates the approximate area under the speed-time curve by dividing the total time into 12 intervals.

2) Doubles the number of intervals, recomputes the area, and compares the two areas.

3) Continues to double the number of intervals until the change in area due to doubling the number of intervals is less than 0.1%.

4) Prints out the results.

B. Write a program in BASIC to implement the flow chart produced above.

PROJECT 6 WORLD DYNAMICS SIMULATION

You are now well aware that a computer is capable of handling large quantities of information and a computer program can be written to simulate the behavior of various scientific and technological phenomena. In a similar fashion, economists, engineers, political scientists, demographers, and others use a computer to simulate the behavior of very large interacting systems, e.g., the world's population, industrial output, food production, resource utilization, pollution generation and health care. In such a simulation the intent is not so much to predict the condition of the world in the future as it is to demonstrate how the future condition depends upon the present assumptions, traditions and policy decisions. Generally a number of computer runs are made with different assumptions so that influence (or lack of influence) of variables upon each other can be observed. Each different run is sometimes called a scenario. For this project we shall write a simplified world model computer program. It should be emphasized that the difficulty of such simulations is not the writing of the sometimes rather complex program, but rather the ability to obtain reliable facts that describe the relationships among the various interacting components of the system.

The Model

We wish to simulate the average population and industrial (or capital) output of the world starting in the year 1975 based upon historical patterns that have prevailed over the past approximately 75 years. This model will be a simplified version of that discussed in the book, "The Limits to Growth," by Meadows et al (1972). This book is an excellent discussion of the concepts and results of such a world model computer simulation. To describe the behavior in time of the population, industrial output (or capital) and natural resource reserves we, of course, need information on birth and death rates, rates of generation of new capital and loss of old (depreciation), utilization of natural (non-renewable) resources and possibility of discovering additional resources.

In a small time increment, I, the change in population, capital and resources may be written:

$$\Delta P = (B - M) * P * I \tag{1}$$

$$\Delta C = (G - D) * C * I \tag{2}$$

$$\Delta R = F * R * I - U * P * I \tag{3}$$

where

P = population/(population in 1975)

C = capital/(capital in 1975)

R = resources/(resources in 1975)

B = annual per capita birth rate

M = annual per capita death (mortality) rate

G = annual percentage growth of capital

D = annual depreciation rate

U = annual per capita resource utilization rate

F = annual percentage increase in resources due to discovery

The functions B, M, G, D, U and F are, of course, not constants but depend upon the conditions of the world. The dependencies presented below have been adapted from "The Limits to Growth" and represent the patterns that seem to have been governing the world up to the present time.

Birth Rates and Mortality Rates

The per capita birth rate seems to be correlated best with the per capita industrial output C/P. At very low C/P there is inadequate food and medical care so that the birth rate is low; at somewhat higher C/P there is a tendency for more births to compensate for the poor survival of children to adulthood. The maximum attainable birth rate is approximately 55 per thousand. Finally at high C/P the birth rate becomes lower apparently reflecting the attitudes of potential parents having a higher standard of living. As expected mortality rates continue to drop with increasing C/P until the standard of living is such that completely adequate health care and nutrition are available. The Table below gives these birth and death rates as a function of the C/P ratio.

Birth and Death Rates

C/P	0	.025	.05	.125	.25	.5	1.0	1.25	2.50	5	10	>10
Births per 1000	0	1	10	30	55	45	39	30	20	18	15	15
Deaths per 1000	1000	1000	300	100	55	40	20	19	15	15	15	15

Notes

1975 WORLD AVERAGE VALUE CORRESPONDS TO C/P = 1
U.S.A. has C/P = 7; Western Europe, C/P = 2 − 5; India C/P = .4

NON-RENEWABLE RESOURCES

Our model lumps all resources together although they obviously are utilized at different rates and different amounts of reserves are available, e.g., at current rates petroleum resources may last 20–40 years while coal may last 1,000–2,000 years. Our model takes a single aggregate resource that would have a lifetime of 250 years at current use rates assuming no additional discoveries occurred. In fact, we shall assume that the resource will grow at a rate of 1% per year by new discoveries and that it cannot decrease to less than 2% of its 1975 value. The per capita utilization rate is definitely a function of the standard of living as measured by C/P. The Table below gives the function as adapted from "Limits to Growth".

Per Capita Resource Utilization Rate

C/P	0	.025	.05	.125	.25	.5	1.0	1.25	2.50	5	10	>10
U	0	.0001	.0002	.0005	.001	.0025	.004	.006	.015	.020	.025	.025

Capital and Industrial Growth

A portion of all industrial output is traditionally reinvested to create new capital for further growth in equipment, factories, etc., which generate new output and more capital. We shall model this generation of new capital by the function G which is the annual percent increase in capital. This growth function is expected to decrease as resources become scarce reflecting the increased costs of extraction of the resources. We shall assume the following form:

Percent Growth in Capital

R	>.7	.7 – .3	.3 – .1	<.1
G	12	9	5	1

Capital Equipment also wears out and must be replaced. To model this we shall assume a fixed depreciation rate of 8% per year.

Project

You are to write a program in BASIC that simulates the behavior of the world for the next 200 years according to the above model. Your output should be in the form of a table of variables such as population, capital, C/P and resources as a function of time. You may also plot the results. After you have run this base case make some modifications in the model's assumptions to attempt to provide improved stability in the world, a higher standard of living and conservation of resources. It would be reasonable to attempt to find a policy that will provide a world average C/P greater than 2, i.e., a standard of living similar to Western Europe in 1975.

Some possible changes might be to invoke ZPG (zero population growth) after X years, restrict capital growth, decrease utilization rates by improved recycling, etc. You should run at least 3 modified models. For each modification you make you must clearly state the assumptions you are using.

Note: Although the simple model presented above is as realistic as possible, there are a number of criticisms that should be made.

(1) It doesn't include the influence of pollution on health and its relation to industrial output. (See "Limits to Growth.")

(2) The relationships between variables are much more complex than depicted here. We have only considered the most important relationships. (See "Limits to Growth.")

(3) A more accurate model would not consider the average behavior of the world, but should look at regions of the world having similar characteristics. A later book, "Mankind at the Turning Point" describes such a model.

(4) Finally, it would be well to point out some philosophic criticism. See the book, "The Doomsday Syndrome" by John Maddox, 1972.

PROJECT 7   SIMULATION OF THE RHINE TEST FOR ESP

Introduction

Experimenters in the field of extrasensory perception (ESP) have for many years used an experiment involving a deck of (25) cards comprised of 5 identical cards in each of 5 "suits" represented by symbols. After shuffling the deck, the subject is asked to name the suit of each card in turn, prior to revealing the identity of the card. Some subjects make appreciably higher scores than others, and they are sometimes judged to have ESP. Experimenters with ESP often reason that if the subject guessed at random then a match should occur, on the average, once in 5 tries. Hence, the number of matches expected for the entire deck would be 5. If a subject scores higher than 5 on such a test, this might be taken as prima facie evidence of some type of thought transmission process (or other form of ESP). However, the interpretation of the results of such tests can be very risky. It is important, therefore, to understand how the results of such tests are influenced if the subject makes random guesses or if he employs some kind of "strategy". This is the objective of this Project.

The Problem

Write a program to compute the empirical (experimental) distribution of scores on the ESP test described above (by simulating the experiment a large number of times) if the results are based on chance alone. (It is recommended that you perform at least one ESP experiment with a deck of cards prior to writing your computer program for simulating the proposed ESP test.) The program should be organized and written in the following manner:

1. Write a routine to simulate the shuffling of a deck of 25 cards by scrambling 25 symbols. After checking this routine, convert it to a subroutine.

2. Write a routine which will simulate the guesses made by a subject. Assume that the subject does not remember guesses made previously nor does he remember the identity of cards shown previously. (Hence, he makes 25 <u>independent</u> choices from among the 5 suits.) Convert this routine to a subroutine.

3. Write a routine that will compare the guesses made by a subject to the psychologist's shuffled deck and will count the number of matches achieved. The routine should also tally the number of subjects that have made each of the possible number of matches. Convert this routine to a subroutine.

4. Write a main program that uses the subroutines described above to conduct L experiments, printing out the cumulative results after every C experiments. (For debugging purposes, L and C should be set to a small number, say 1. For the actual simulation, let L = 1000 and C = 100.)

5. Write another subroutine to simulate the guesses made by a subject who keeps track (mentally?) of his guesses to insure that each suit is guessed only 5 times. Incorporate this subroutine into the main program by letting it replace (2). Proceed again as indicated in (4). Discuss whether or not this "strategy" has any significant influence on the test results. If possible, give an explanation for the results obtained.

6. Based on (2) and (5), what criterion would you recommend for the determination of whether or not a subject "has ESP"?

Possible extensions:

7. Write another subroutine to simulate the guesses made by a (clever?) subject who keeps track of the cards which have already been shown and who guesses from among the suits with the greatest number remaining in the deck. Comment as to whether or not this "strategy" has a significant effect on the results. Can you provide an explanation for these results?

8. Based on (2), (5), and (7), what criterion would you recommend for the determination of whether or not a subject "has ESP"?

What other "strategies" can you devise?

PROJECT 8 COMPUTER DATING

The Isaac Love University (affectionately known as I. Love U.) has recently become a coeducational institution. Simultaneously, Love has undergone a considerable expansion (in enrollment). The faculty and administration at Love University have traditionally concerned themselves with the total contentment and well-being of the students. One of the potential problems brought on by coeducation and expansion is the increased difficulty experienced by students of one sex in meeting satisfactory members of the opposite sex. Since the ensuing frustrations created by this problem might lead to a deterioration in the student's normally optimistic outlook on life, finding a suitable date is considered Love's number one problem.

You, as an expert in writing BASIC computer programs, have been engaged by the Dean of Love to develop a computer dating program, which will be called MINIMATCH. In order to guide you in your task, the Love counsellors have come up with a series of specifications which must be met by your program. They are as follows:

Love's Minimum Specifications

1. The program must be capable of handling up to 50 names, total.

2. The number of males and females need not be the same, but their combined total must not exceed the amount stated in 1.

3. The program must be capable of handling names up to fifteen letters long (including initials, periods, etc.), if necessary.

4. All females will be compared with all males, and vice versa, before the program computes the first and second choice dates for each. Note, one individual might be the first or second choice of more than one member of the opposite sex, while one might end up being no one's first or second choice.

5. Compatability of the proposed dates is to be determined from data established from a 10-part (minimum) questionnaire to be developed by you or like the one on page 168. This questionnaire is to have 5 information responses about the applicant, and 5 preference responses about potential dates. Each preference response should relate to a corresponding information response. For example:

Information Statement				*Response*		
	∅	1	2	3	4	5
Your recreational interests are best described by which of the following categories (fractions, such as 2.3, may be used)	Meditation, Prayer, etc.	Reading, Writing, etc.	Playing Chess, Checkers, Cards, etc.	Dancing, Picnics, Walks, Fishing, etc.	Surfing, Jogging, Hiking, Tennis, Football, etc.	Skydiving, Racing Stock Cars, etc.

Preference Statement				*Response*		
	∅	1	2	3	4	5
Which of the categories best describes what you would like your date to be interested in (fractions, such as 2.3, may be used)	Meditation, Prayer, etc.	Reading, Writing, etc.	Playing Chess, Checkers, Cards, etc.	Dancing, Picnics, Walks, Fishing, etc.	Surfing, Jogging, Hiking, Tennis, Football, etc.	Skydiving, Racing Stock Cars, etc.

Notice that the various response categories within a particular statement should be so arranged that they range more-or-less uniformly from one extreme to another (i.e., in the example, the response categories range from introverted action to extroverted action). There need not always be the same number of response categories for each statement, but a particular information statement should have the same categories as the corresponding preference statement. The ultimate success of the entire program depends upon the validity of the questionnaire response listings.

6. First and second choice dates are determined by computing the total units of difference where an applicant's preference responses are compared with the corresponding information responses of all members of the opposite sex. The one with the least mismatch (therefore greatest compatability) will become the first choice date, while the next least mismatch

becomes the second choice date. In case of tie scores, you may use any criteria (i.e., random, alphabetical etc.) to determine which date is specified.

7. All data from the questionnaires is to be placed in DATA statements (beginning with line 9000, one line for each applicant) using the following format:

9XXX DATA "NAME",   "M/F", $\underline{N0}$, $\underline{N1}$, $\underline{N2}$ . . . . . , $\underline{N9}$

where

    Name = applicant's name (15 characters max.)

    M/F = applicant's sex (male/female)

    N0 through N9 = ten response numbers for the ten questionnaire statements.

8. The program you write is to point out a final table using the following format:

FEMALES:

Name	First Choice	Second Choice
Name 1	Date 1	Date 2
.	.	.
.	.	.
.	.	.

MALES:

Name	First Choice	Second Choice
Name 1	Date 1	Date 2
.	.	.
.	.	.
.	.	.

The name lists are to be in alphabetical order, even when the DATA order is mixed and not in alphabetical order. This means your program must alphabetize both lists, and must be able to break the data down into two lists.

Your job as computer consultant is to use the above Love constraints to develop a complete report containing the following (not necessarily in the given order):

1. Sample questionnaire

2. Listing of complete program

3. Sample run of program for ten applicants

4. Short writeup explaining your MINIMATCH

5. Conclusions and recommendations

6. Anything else you feel appropriate

Isaac Love University

Department of Extracurricular Activities

Minimatch Questionnaire

As a member of the student body of Isaac Love University, you are being asked to answer the following questions to aid us in finding you the ideal date.

NAME_____

SEX_____

1. Your recreational interests are best described by which of the following categories (fractions, such as 2.3, may be used):

$\emptyset$	1	2	3	4	5
meditation, prayer, etc.	reading, writing, etc.	playing chess, checkers, cards, etc.	dancing, picnics, walks	surfing, jogging, tennis, football	skydiving, racing stock cars

Answer_____

2. Your reading interests are best described by the following categories:

$\emptyset$	1	2	3	4
Churchill's History of the Second World War (in six volumes)	James Joyce Shakespeare Nabakov	Michener Steinbeck Hemingway	Ian Fleming Earle Stanely Gardner	Charles Shultz Superman Comics

Answer_____

3. The movies you attend are usually rated:

$\emptyset$	1	2	3
G	GP	R	X

Answer_____

4. The music you like is best described as:

$\emptyset$	1	2	3
Opera	Classical	Popular, Country	Rock, Soul

Answer_____

5. Which category most nearly represents your taste in food:

1	2	3
Hamburger, Hot dog	Steak or roast beef	Beef Wellington, chateaubriand

Answer_____

6. Which category best describes what you would like your date's interests to be?

$\emptyset$	1	2	3	4	5
meditation, prayer, etc.	reading, writing, etc.	playing chess, checkers, cards, etc.	dancing, picnics, walks	surfing, jogging, tennis, football	skydiving, racing stock cars

Answer_____

7. Which category would you like your date to read:

$\emptyset$	1	2	3	4
Churchill's History of the Second World War (in six volumes)	James Joyce Shakespeare Nabakov	Michener Steinbeck Hemingway	Ian Fleming Earle Stanley Gardner	Charles Shultz Superman Comics

Answer_____

8. The rating of the movies you would prefer your date attended falls in which category:

$\emptyset$	1	2	3
G	GP	R	X

Answer_____

9. Which kind of music would you like your date to be interested in:

$\emptyset$	1	2	3
Opera	Classical	Popular, Country	Rock, Soul

Answer_____

10. Which kind of food would you like your date to prefer:

1	2	3
Hamburger, Hot dog	Steak or roast beef	Beef Wellington, chateaubriand

Answer_____

PROJECT 9   THE PORSCHE 917 RACE CAR

The purpose of this project is to simulate the acceleration profile of a Group 5 sports car—a Porsche-Type 917. The car is under the influence of various external forces, depending on engine output, aerodynamic drag, and rolling friction. This motion is determined by the laws of Newtonian mechanics. Hence, the motion of the car can be simulated on the computer in order to observe the changes in motion under different conditions.

Consider first the simple situation of a car of mass M, initially at rest, acted on by force F. The force F, produced by the engine driving the rear wheels, produces an acceleration A, given by:

$$F = M * A \qquad (1)$$

or

$$A = F/M \qquad (2)$$

The acceleration produced by the force generated by the engine can be used to determine the velocity and distance travelled at any given time. To simulate the motion, we use small time intervals of length I. Suppose that the simulation has proceeded for N time intervals, and at time T1 (T1 = N * I) the velocity is V and the distance traveled is S. The new velocity V and the new distance travelled S at the end of each time interval I can be determined in the following manner:

Since the acceleration is the rate of change of velocity,
the velocity at the end of the time interval is given by

$$V \leftarrow V + A * I \qquad (3)$$

└─── velocity at beginning of time interval I

└─── new velocity at end of time interval I

Similarly, since the velocity is the rate of change of distance travelled, the distance travelled at the end of the time interval is given by

$$S \leftarrow S + V * I \hspace{4cm} (4)$$

distance at beginning of time interval I

distance at end of time interval I

The velocity used in equation (4) may be either the velocity at the beginning of time interval I or at the end of the time interval. In practice, the time interval is chosen to be sufficiently small such that the difference is negligible, and we will adopt the convention that the velocity is always altered before the distance. Essentially, we have broken the continuous motion of the car into a series of very small intervals and approximated the motion in each interval. The smaller we choose our time interval I, the better will be our approximation of the motion until round-off and truncation errors become substantial.

Two other forces acting on the car must be considered during acceleration, viz; aerodynamic drag D and the rolling friction R. We will assume the race track is flat so that the gravitational force does not enter the problem. The rolling friction will be assumed to be a constant force acting to decelerate the car. The aerodynamic drag D also tends to decelerate the car and is expressed as

$$D = K * V * V \hspace{4cm} (5)$$

where

K is the drag coefficient (constant)

V is the speed of the car

Now, at any time T, the total force acting on the car is

$$F_T = F_R - D - R \hspace{3.5cm} (6)$$

where

F_T = total force at time T

F_R = engine force delivered to rear wheels

R = rolling friction

The engine speed is determined by the selection of the gear ratio in the transmission and by the velocity of the car. Assume that this car has four gear ratios available. The engine speed E can be determined as follows:

$$E = V * 59.677/G \ (N) \qquad (7)$$

where

E = Engine speed in RPM

V = Velocity of the car in m/s

G (N) = Gear ratio

N = Integer (1, 2, 3, or 4) designating 1st, 2nd, 3rd, or 4th gears

The engine force delivered through the rear wheels is determined by the gear ratio as

$$F_R = F_E \ / \ G \ (N) \qquad (8)$$

where

F_E is the output force of the engine

Problem Description:

Assume the following specifications for the car:

M = Mass of car = 807 kg

R = Rolling friction = 118 Newtons

K = Drag coefficient = 0.36 (to give drag in Newtons when V is in m/s) The engine produces roughly 630 brake horsepower at 8300 rpm

The maximum torque is 569 Newton-meters at 6300 rpm. The gear ratios in the 4-speed transmission are:

$$G(1) = .25$$
$$G(2) = .5$$
$$G(3) = .6$$
$$G(4) = .7$$

The engine speed must not exceed 9000 rpm.

The speed-dependence of the engine output force is shown on the accompanying figure (page 176).

The engine output force is nonlinear. However, a nonlinear curve can be approximated by a series of linear segments, i.e., straight lines, with each segment accurate only over a certain speed range. (The accuracy of the approximation can be improved by increasing the number of line segments.) Each line segment is represented by the equation

$$F_E = F_x + C_x * (E - E_x)$$

where

X = segment which corresponds to the particular engine speed

F_E = output force of engine (Newtons)

C_x = conversion factor (Newton/rpm)

E = engine speed (rpm)

E_x = lowest engine speed (rpm) represented by this line segment

The engine output curve has been divided into five straight line segments which can be described as follows:

SPEED (rpm)	RANGE (rpm)	F_x (Newton)	Cx (Newton/rpm)	Ex (rpm)
0 ≤ E < 2000		2380.4	+0.357	0
2000 ≤ E < 4000		3094.4	+0.186	2000
4000 ≤ E < 6300		3466.4	+0.04	4000
6300 ≤ E < 7500		3558.4	−0.3	6300
7500 ≤ E <		3198.4	−1.2	7500

For example, if the engine is running at 3500 rpm, the output force of the engine would be

$$F_E = 3094.4 + .186* (3500 - 2000)$$
$$F_E = 3373.4 \text{ Newtons}$$

At any time, the driver has one of four gear ratios available to drive the rear wheels of the car. He will select the gear which transmits the greatest force to the rear wheels (in order to achieve the maximum possible acceleration and final speed).

Example 1:

If the car is traveling at 17.881 m/s (40 mph), then there are four possible engine speeds, depending on the gear ratio selected. Using Equation (7) and the following gear ratios

$$G(1) = 0.25 \qquad G(2) = 0.5 \qquad G(3) = 0.6 \qquad G(4) = 0.7$$

one obtains:

$$E(1) = 17.8811* 59.677/.25 = 4268.36 \text{ RPM}$$
$$E(2) = 17.8811* 59.677/ .5 = 2134.18 \text{ RPM}$$
$$E(3) = 17.8811* 59.677/ .6 = 1778.48 \text{ RPM}$$
$$E(4) = 17.8811* 59.677/ .7 = 1524.41 \text{ RPM}$$

The force transmitted to the rear wheels is found from the approximation to the force-speed curve, together with equation (8), and gives the following results:

$$F_R (1) = (3466.4 + .04 * (4268.36 - 4000)) /.25 = 13908.54 \text{ Newtons}$$
$$F_R (2) = (3094.4 + .186 * (2134.18 - 2000)) /.5 = 6238.71 \text{ Newtons}$$
$$F_R (3) = (2380.4 + .357 * (1778.48 - 0)) /.6 = 5025.53 \text{ Newtons}$$
$$F_R (4) = (2380.4 + .357 * (1524.41 - 0)) /.7 = 4178.02 \text{ Newtons}$$

Therefore, in order to maximize the propulsive force at 40 mph, the transmission should be in 1st gear with an engine speed of approximately 4268 rpm.

Example 2:

At 67.054 m/s (V= 150 mph),

$$F_R(1) = 0 \text{ (Engine speed greater}$$

E(1) = 16006.32 rpm   than 9000 rpm)

E(2) = 8003.16 rpm $F_R(2) = 5189.21$ Newtons

E(3) = 6669.30 rpm $F_R(3) = 5746.01$ Newtons

E(4) = 5716.54 rpm $F_R(4) = 5050.09$ Newtons

At 150 mph the transmission should be in 3rd gear with an engine speed of approximately 6669 rpm.

After the force transmitted to the rear wheels is maximized (by selecting the appropriate gear position), the dynamic variables are given by:

$$A = (F_R - D - R)/M$$
$$V \leftarrow V + A * I$$
$$S \leftarrow S + V * I$$

At any time the gear ratio is changed, the force transmitted to the rear wheels is reduced to zero ($F_R = 0$) for a time period equal to the time it takes the driver to shift gears. During this period, the dynamic variables are given by:

$$A = (-D - R)/M$$
$$V = V + A * I$$
$$S = S + V * I$$

Project Requirements:

A.   Determine the optimum times (to the nearest 1/16 s) at which the gears should be shifted and the engine speed necessary to match the car velocity when the new gear is engaged. Assume it takes 1/4 s to shift gears. Use a value for I = 1/16 s. Determine also the time in seconds and the distance in meters it takes for the car to attain a speed of 330 KPH, starting from rest.

B.   Recompute Part A with a drag coefficient of 0.46.

C.   Re-run Part A with a drag coefficient of 0.36 and I = 1/32 s.

D.   To make the simulation more realistic, you may wish to include
the power lost in the engine, gear box, drive masses and wheels
during acceleration. These losses depend on the gear and estimates
are as follows

Gear	Power Loss
1st	41%
2nd	34%
3rd	22%
4th	12%

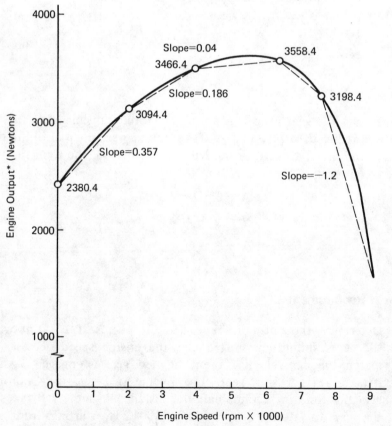

PORSCHE–TYPE 917
5 Liter, Air-Cooled Flat 12, Borsch Injection

*Compensated for a rearend ratio of 0.35 and tire diameter of 0.91 metres

PROJECT 10 QUEUING

Introduction

A precise definition of simulation is difficult to obtain. The term is used to cover a wide variety of activities ranging from the development of mathematical relations describing a system, to the construction of a physical model or mock-up. For the purposes of this project, the term simulation will be used to describe the process of formulating a suitable mathematical model of a system, the development of a computer program to solve the equations of the model, and operation of the computer to determine values for system variables.

The emphasis will be on the computer aspects of the process and the phrases "modeling" and "simulation" will be encountered. Although this seems to imply that modeling is not a part of simulation, this is not the case. Modeling is a very important phase of the simulation process. Modeling involves the development of mathematical relations describing the system variables. Since the equations of the model are the basis for simulation, the results are only as good as the model.

The first stage in the design of a simulation is to make a mathematical model of the process. Two types of models can be used to describe a process, viz., a deterministic model or a probabilistic model. For example, Newton's laws of classical mechanics are a mathematical model which governs the dynamics of the motion of an object. Such a model is deterministic in that the characteristics of the motion, e.g., the displacement, the velocity, and the acceleration, are determined by equations. However, it is not always possible to make such a model of a real process. Consider the simple operation of flipping a coin. Although Newtonian mechanics should predict whether the coin will land heads or tails (given the initial velocity, spin, height, etc.), in practice it is impossible to determine this in advance. Consequently, a deterministic model cannot be used. Instead, we can make a probabilistic model of this process by noting that the probability that the coin lands heads equals one half. Although such models will not determine precisely what will happen, a great deal can be learned about the physical process by studying such models. For example, the landing and take-off of aircraft at an airport, the traffic patterns in a city, or the motion (position and velocity) of molecules in a gas all have an uncertainty in them. In such problems, we cannot say for certain that a particular event will occur; at best we can assign or estimate the probability of an event happening. Nevertheless, some engineering problems have this character and must still be analyzed to obtain useful results.

One way of modeling such processes is to assign appropriate probabilities based upon past experience or theoretical considerations and then to replicate the process many times using a computer. We then presume that the average of many such trials should be a reasonable estimate of how the process will behave. This technique is often called a Monte Carlo method.

Problem — Single Server Queuing System

The system to be simulated is a single channel queuing system such as the check-out system in a supermarket or a tool crib in a machine shop or a ticket stand at the movies. Customers (units) arrive in a random fashion and enter service if there is no unit in the system. If there is already one or more units in the system, the arriving unit joins the waiting line.

The arrival time is obtained by noting when a customer arrives into the system. The inter-arrival time is the time elapsed between successive arrivals. The time at which service begins for the nth customer will be the larger of the arrival time of the nth customer and the time at which service ends for the customer presently being serviced. The service time is the difference between the times at which service begins and ends. The time spent in the waiting line is obtained by subtracting the arrival time from the time at which service begins. Similarly, the time spent in the system is obtained by subtracting the arrival time from the time at which service ends. Dividing the number of arrivals by the time the facility is open to receive arrivals, we obtain

$$\text{Arrival rate, A} = \frac{\text{number of arrivals}}{\text{time facility is open for arrivals}}$$

Dividing the total time spent servicing customers by the number of customers serviced, we obtain

$$\text{Average service time, S} = \frac{\text{total service time}}{\text{number served}}$$

Taking the reciprocal of average service time, we obtain

$$\text{Service rate, R} = \frac{1}{S}$$

Dividing the total time spent waiting by all customers by the number of customers,
   observed average time spent in waiting line,

$$W_q = \frac{\text{Total waiting time}}{\text{Number of customers}}$$

Similarly,
   observed average time spent in system,

$$W = \frac{\text{Total time in system}}{\text{Number of customers}}$$

Problems of this type have been shown to have distributions for inter-arrival times (times to next arrival) given by

$$x = -\ln (R.N.)/A$$

where R.N. is a random number between 0 and 1, A is the arrival rate, ln stands for natural logarithm and x is a random inter-arrival time.
   Similarly, the service time distribution can be simulated by

$$y = -\ln (R.N._1 * R.N._2)/2R$$

where $R.N._1$ and $R.N._2$ are independent random numbers between 0 and 1, R is the service rate, and y is a random service time.
   The program starts by initializing the variables and determining the first arrival time. Since there is no one in the system, the next discharge time is set to a large number. Next a test is made to determine if the next event is an arrival or discharge. (The first time through the program the next event must be an arrival.) Clocks which keep track of arrival times, service times, and total time in system are updated as are the number in the queue. If there is no one presently being serviced, the arrival gets serviced using a computed service time. If there is currently someone in the system, the arrival is added to the waiting line, and the next event is determined, after checking stopping criteria.

After a discharge, the number in the system is decreased and the total number serviced (throughout) is increased. Again, stopping criteria are checked and the next event is branched to.

Problem

1. Write a program that will simulate the arrivals and service of customers at a single check-out supermarket. The program should provide the running of up to 1000 arrivals and varying service and arrival times.

2. Run your program for a mean arrival rate of 20 customers/hour and a mean service rate of 20 served/hour. Print out the number of customers, the mean arrival rate, the mean service time, the average number of customers in the system, the average time spent in the system, and the average waiting time.

3. Discuss your results including

    a. How many customers must be simulated to get reliable answers?

    b. What is the effect of decreasing service times (i.e., lower mean service time) on the waiting queue?

PROJECT 11 DETERMINATION OF ROOTS AND EXTREMA

Introduction

There are many examples in business, science and engineering where a quantity of interest can be expressed as a function of one or more variables. Furthermore, one is very often interested in the values of the independent variable for which the function may vanish. Such problems involve the determination of the roots of an equation and the determination of any extreme values (maxima or minima) which the function may have. Finding the root of an equation is a problem of far-reaching practical importance. In its simplest form, this problem is usually restricted to finding the points at which a polynominal with rational coefficients is equal to zero. Even this task is far from trivial; if the degree of the polynominal is greater than 4, there is no general formula for the roots.

We are interested in the more general problem of finding the real roots of an equation of the form $f(V) = 0$ where f may be any function definable in BASIC. A particularly simple method is described in Chapter 8. Application of this method to the aircraft problem described below should not only provide a useful application of the capabilities of the computer, but also should provide a useful physical insight into the real nature of roots and extrema and to their determination.

Discussion

Any aircraft remains airborne by creating a lifting force at least as great as its weight. For conventional fixed-wing vehicles (as opposed to rotary-wing vehicles such as helicopters), this lift generation requires a relatively high forward speed. However, such motion is accompanied by resistance, or drag, which must be overcome by the thrust of the propulsion system, e.g., an engine propeller, gas turbine, or rocket. The "flight envelope" of each aircraft is that range of flight speeds over which the propulsive thrust available is equal to or greater than the thrust required to overcome the drag and remain airborne.

At low flight speeds, the creation of the required lift necessitates placing the aircraft in a nose-up attitude, thus producing a rearward component of the lifting force which is called "drag due to lift" (D_1); this is inversely proportional to the square of the flight speed V, i.e.,

$$D_1 = A/V^2$$

At moderate subsonic flight speeds, the primary contribution to the drag comes from frictional resistance; and this contribution (D_2) is proportional to the square of the flight speed, i.e.,

$$D_2 = BV^2$$

At very high flight speeds, the formation of shock waves about the aircraft (the cause of sonic booms) results in a contribution (D_3) to the drag which is an exponential function of the flight speed, i.e.,

$$D_3 = C \exp (V/K)$$

The total drag (D) of the aircraft is the sum of the three contributions described above, i.e.,

$$D = D_1 + D_2 + D_3$$

or

$$D (V) = A/V^2 + BV^2 + C \exp (V/K)$$

In general, the thrust available (T) is a function of flight speed (V). However, for many aircraft propulsion systems, the thrust available is independent of flight speed over a wide range of operational speeds. Assuming this to be the case for the commercial aircraft of current interest, the excess thrust available (E) is given by

$$E (V) = T - D (V)$$
$$= T - [A/V^2 + BV^2 + C \exp (V/K)]$$

It is evident, that in order for the aircraft to maintain a constant flight speed, the thrust must equal the drag. Consequently, the maximum drag cannot exceed the maximum thrust available. Clearly, the maximum drag occurs at some minimum speed (V_1), due to the contribution D_1, and at some maximum speed (V_2), due to the contributions D_2 and D_3. Finally, it is evident that a critical flight speed V^* exists ($V_1 < V^* < V_2$) at which the excess thrust has its maximum value. (Of course, this is the flight speed at which the drag is minimum.)

Problem

Consider the Boeing 737 aircraft, which contains two Pratt & Whitney JT-8D turbofan engines, each of which can provide up to 12,500 lbs. of continuous thrust. Wind tunnel tests have indicated that the drag parameters (A, B, D, K, described above) for the Boeing 737 are:

$$A = 2.42 \times 10^8 \text{ lb (mph)}^2$$
$$B = 0.07 \text{ lb/(mph)}^2$$
$$C = 1.66 \text{ lb}$$
$$K = 70 \text{ mph}$$

(a) Compute the minimum and maximum flight speeds to the closest 1 mph using an iterative method of root solving.

(b) Compute (to the closest 1 mph) the flight speed at which the excess thrust available has its maximum value. It is possible to use the same iterative method of root solving as in (a) above.

(c) As a qualitative check of your results, produce a computer plot of the flight speed-dependence of the excess thrust over the speed range 50 to 600 mph.

PROJECT 12   OPTIMIZATION BY LINEAR PROGRAMMING

Frequently, it is necessary to determine the conditions of operation of a plant or process that will optimize some criterion such as production rate, profit, cost, or environmental impact. If such a goal can be expressed in a quantitative way, i.e., mathematically, there are a large number of mathematical techniques (optimization methods) that can be used to determine the "best" conditions of operation. The quantitative expression of a desired goal is known as the objective function in optimization theory.

Linear Programming

In optimization problems, one is concerned with choosing the optimum solution to a problem from a number of possible (or feasible) solutions. The best solution is that which maximizes or minimizes the objective function, subject to any imposed conditions or constraints on the values that the variables may take. In linear programming problems, the objective function is a <u>linear</u> function of the independent variables. In addition, all constraints are expressed mathematically either as <u>linear</u> equalities or <u>linear</u> inequalities. (A linear inequality is a linear equation in which the equality sign has been replaced by an inequality sign.)

Example 1

Suppose we wish to find the values of X_1 and X_2 that make the objective function $(2X_1 + 4X_2)$ as large as possible, subject to the following constraints:

$$X_1 \geqslant 0$$
$$X_2 \geqslant 0$$
$$X_1 + X_2 \leqslant 2$$

If we sketch the constraints on a X_1, X_2 plane they define a feasible region in which an acceptable solution exists as shown in Figure 1A on page 189. Now sketch in lines corresponding to the equation $(2X_1 + 4X_2) = C$, i.e., the objective function corresponding to various values.

(Figure 1B) It is clear that the largest value of the objective function, when X_1 and X_2 still lie in the feasible region, is 8 when $X_1 = 0$ and $X_2 = 2$. Hence, the optimum operating conditions for this problem are $X_1 = 0$, $X_2 = 2$. Note that the optimum value occurred on the boundary of the feasible region. This will always be the case in linear problems.

Example 2

A small machine shop manufactures two items, Grenches and Folts, by using a grinder and a polisher according to the following schedule:

	Grinder	*Polisher*	*Profit*
Grenches	4 hrs.	1 hr.	$4
Folts	3 hrs.	3 hrs.	$6

The shop works a 36 hour week, and 4 grinders and 3 polishers are available. Assuming that all of the items produced can be sold, how many of each product should be manufactured in order to maximize the profit?

The first step in solving this problem (or any one like it) is to introduce a notation which enables the problem to be stated clearly in mathematical form. Accordingly, let A denote the weekly production of Grenches, B the weekly production of Folts, and P the profit, given by $ (4A + 6B). Note that the total time available on the grinders each week is 144 hours, while 108 hours of polishing time are provided. The problem can be stated mathematically in the following way:

$$\text{Maximize } 4A + 6B$$

$$\text{subject to} \qquad A \geqslant 0 \qquad\qquad (1)$$

$$B \geqslant 0 \qquad\qquad (2)$$

$$4A + 3B \leqslant 144 \qquad\qquad (3)$$

$$A + 3B \leqslant 108 \qquad\qquad (4)$$

The inequalities above, called the constraints of the problem, are shown graphically in Figure 2A. Inequalities (1) and (2) insure that whatever quantity of Grenches and Folts are selected by management, the shop will not be required to manufacture a negative quantity of either! Inequalities (3) and (4) express respectively, the restrictions imposed on the weekly manufacturing scheme by the amount of grinding and polishing time available. The constraints, all of which must be satisfied simultaneously, define a feasible region shown in Figure 2A. Only those points (A, B) in this feasible region can be considered when searching for the combinations which provide the maximum profit. Lines corresponding to various values of the profit P ($4A + 6B = P$) are shown in Figure 2B, indicating that some values of P are attainable while others are not. The solution to the problem is easily determined graphically by moving a line of appropriate constant slope ($-2/3$) across the feasible region, until the value of P cannot be increased any further without leaving the feasible region. For this problem, the maximum profit attainable is \$240 corresponding to 12 Grenches and 32 Folts. Note that the optimum solution occurred not only on the boundary of the feasible region, but also at a corner point corresponding to the intersection of two of the constraint equations. Since this is generally true in linear programming problems, we are now in a position to generalize (without proof) a technique for solving linear programming problems.

The general linear programming problem can be stated in the following way:

> Given a set of m linear equations or inequalities
> involving n variables, find the non-negative values
> of these variables which satisfy the equations and
> inequalities and also maximize or minimize a linear
> objective function.

The solution of the linear problem is found only at one of several specific locations called <u>extreme points</u>. The extreme points are defined by the constraints on the problem and are relatively few in number. A calculation of the objective function at each of the extreme points (intersections) enables one to choose the optimum value from among these few choices.

In a two-variable problem, the solution is easily obtained by the graphical procedures employed in the previous examples. For problems with more than two variables, however, the solution is not easily obtained geometrically. Nevertheless, the following procedure is a valid (although not the most sophisticated) method of solution. For an n-variable problem:

1. Calculate the intersection points by solving simultaneously all possible combinations of the m equality constraint equations taken n at a time.

2. Check to see which intersection points satisfy all of the constraint equations, i.e., which intersection points represent feasible solutions. These are the extreme points of the problem.

3. Evaluate the objective function at each extreme point and choose the one that provides the largest (or smallest) value of the objective function.

Problem

Imagine that you are employed by the STP Oil Company which purchases crude oil from Arabia, Venezuela and from domestic sources and refines it into three products, viz., aviation fuel, gasoline and fuel oil. The yields of these products from the different crude oils, along with the purchase and processing cost of each crude, is given in Table 1.

TABLE 1

Cost and Yields of Crude Oils [Yield (BBL/BBL)]

Crude	Availability (BBL/day)	Cost ($/Barrel)	Aviation Fuel	Gasoline	Fuel Oil	Waste
Arabian	unlimited	18.50	.15	.50	.30	.05
Venezuelan	60,000	15.00	.15	.60	.25	0
Domestic	120,000	14.00	.10	.40	.40	.10

Also shown in Table 1 is the maximum amount of each of the crudes available per day. The refinery can process no more than 200,000 barrels/day of crude.

The Federal Energy Office (FEO) has not only fixed the prices of the products, but also the minimum amount of each product that must be produced each day. These constraints are given in Table 2. Note that the company is required to produce more gasoline from March to August and more fuel oil from August to March (for apparently obvious reasons).

TABLE 2

Daily Production Minima and Prices (FEO)

Products	Price ($/BBL)	3/1 to 8/1 (BBL)	8/1 to 3/1 (BBL)
Aviation Fuel	25.00	10,000	10,000
Gasoline	19.00	100,000	85,000
Fuel Oil	14.00	50,000	65,000

As a technical expert in the STP Oil Company, your assignment is the following:

1. Formulate the linear programming problem, i.e., write down expressions for the objective function and for the constraints of the problem.

2. Write a computer program which locates the extreme points, evaluates the objective function at these points, and searches these values for the optimum solution. Your program should determine the optimum crude purchasing policy for the refinery for the March-to-August and August-to-March periods.

3. Suppose that at some point Arabian crude is no longer available (embargo). However, the company is able to purchase an unlimited amount of Venezuelan crude for $22.50/BBL (including processing costs). What is the optimum solution under these conditions? Solve this problem analytically (without the computer) or graphically since it is a simple two-variable problem. Does the company have grounds to go to the FEO to obtain either a price increase or a change in production quotas under these circumstances? Why?

4. For additional calculations, you might consider the effect of the crude prices, the production quotas, and the product prices on the optimum solution.

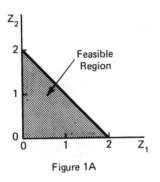

Figure 1A

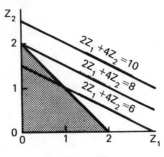

Figure 1B

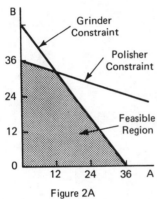

Figure 2A

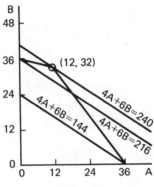

Figure 2B

Appendix A

The Teletype

The input/output device for most systems consists of a keyboard for input and a printer or display for output. Usually these are combined into one unit referred to as a terminal. There are many kinds of terminals each of which is slightly different. The most common terminals are teletypes and video terminals. The teletype is an integrated keyboard and printer which sometimes has additional features such as paper tape readers and punches. Video terminals display the information transmitted to and from the computer on a television like display.

While the keyboards on different terminals vary, we shall discuss only the teletype. All other terminals have the same features on the keyboard so there should be no difficulty locating the corresponding keys on other kinds of terminals. The teletype terminal is very much like a typewriter except it only has upper case letters[†] and some special keys.

Most terminals are connected to the computer via telephone lines. To establish contact, you must dial the computer's telephone number and listen for a high-pitched tone. When you hear the tone, turn the knob on the front of the teletype to "line," place the telephone handset into the teletype coupler, and you are ready to log in. Some terminals are "hard-wired" or physically connected to the computer. For these terminals, simply turn the knob on the front of the teletype to "line". No telephone is involved.

SPECIAL KEYS

1. The backspace key (upper case "o" on the teletype)—This key prints a ← (backward pointing arrow). While the carriage will not

---

[†] There are other types of terminals, besides the teletype, some of which have lower case letters. Note that there are always separate keys for zero and one. A lower case "l" cannot be used for number one, nor can an "o" be used for zero.

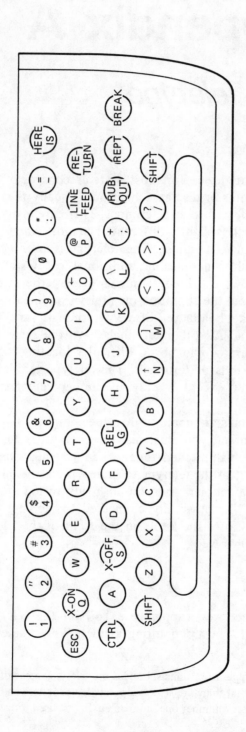

actually backspace*, depressing the (←) will delete the character immediately preceding. Similarly, you can delete two or more characters by hitting the (←) an appropriate number of times. For example, if you type

10   READ ABC ← ←, B, C (return)

the computer will accept this as

10   READ A, B, C

THE BREAK KEY

You can stop the computer from continuing to execute or list a program by depressing the BREAK key on the right hand side of the keyboard. Doing this will interrupt the computer no matter what it is doing. The computer will respond with STOP and will be ready for your next input. You should never interrupt the computer by disconnecting the telephone.

PRODUCING A PAPER TAPE

Since storage space on the computer disk is very limited and since the computer occasionally malfunctions losing the programs stored on the disk, it is often useful to list the program on paper tape. On teletypes equipped with paper tape, just type

PUN

turn the paper tape punch on and then depress the return key. The computer will then list your program on paper and on the paper tape. When it finishes, turn the paper tape punch off.

To read the paper tape, put it in the reader so that the sprocket goes through the line of little holes (they are obvious when you look at a punched paper tape). Close the reader and type

TAPE (return)

---

*On video terminals, the cursor (the line indicating where the next character is typed) actually does backspace.

The computer will respond with a line feed. Push the reader switch to start and the computer will read the paper tape. When it stops, type

KEY (return)

and proceed just as if you had typed the lines in.

A paper tape may be prepared "off line" by turning the teletype to local, the paper tape punch on, and depressing the REPT and RUB OUT keys simultaneously to produce a "leader". Then type your program and REPT and RUB OUT again to produce a "trailer". This tape can then be read on line just as above.

Appendix B

Accessing and Communicating

Every version of BASIC has associated with it a set of commands for getting access to the computer and for communicating with the mass storage device—the disk. These commands are not standard· so we shall describe two typical examples (we shall refer to them as version A and version B). All versions of BASIC will have commands which perform the same functions. Study these examples—then refer to the user's manual for the particular form that these commands take on your system.

VERSION A

Logging In

For time-sharing systems, the user must identify himself—usually by providing a code number and a password.

This is done immediately after establishing contact with the computer. The procedure begins by typing a carriage return and line feed to verify the connection. The computer will respond with either

<u>PLEASE LOG IN</u>

or

<u>???</u>

You then type

HELLO — code number, password (return)

For example

HELLO — A123, XZY (return)

the A123 is the code number and the XZY is the password. After each typed line, the return key must be depressed to transmit that line to the computer.

The computer may print a brief message and finally print

READY

Clearing the CPU

When you have finished with a program and wish to begin a new one, it is necessary to "erase" the old program from the CPU memory. This is done using the command

SCRATCH (return)

Saving a Program

Especially when writing long computer programs, it is not always convenient to write and run a program in one sitting at the terminal. You may wish to have the computer store your program until the next time it is needed. To do this, the program must first be given a name. This is accomplished by typing

NAME — (Name of Program) (return)

The program name may be any combination of 1 to 6 characters[†]. Thus, if you have wanted to name a program SPHERV, just type, for example,

NAME — SPHERV (return)

[†]Some versions reserve some characters such as $ and * for special use so they cannot be used in program names.

A program can be named at anytime while you are working with it. The NAME command can be typed in before, after, or in the middle of typing in the program. Now once a program has been named and you have completed typing it in, it can be saved by typing the command

SAVE (return)

The computer will now save your program by storing it on the disk. It will retain this program for as long as necessary, until you finish with it and instruct the computer to stop saving it. The computer will line-feed, that is, shift to the next line, when it has stored the program.

You may continue to work on a program after typing SAVE. However, any modifications made after the SAVE command will not change the stored version.

Running an Old Program

All systems which allow you to save programs for future use, must of course provide a way to bring them back into the CPU.

To recall a program which has been saved on the disk, type

GET — program name (return)

For example

GET — SAMPLE (return)

This statement clears the CPU of any program or statements which might be there and then copies the desired program from the disk into the CPU. The program is now ready for your use just as if you had typed it in. Note that the computer does not print the program on the terminal. If you wish to review it, (c.f. Chapter 1) use the LIST command.

Eliminating a Saved Program

There are at least two reasons for removing stored programs from the disk. First, disk space is usually very limited and in order to have room for new programs, old programs which are no longer needed must be removed. Second, when changing a program, it is useful to eliminate the old program and save the new version.

To remove a program from the disk, type

PURGE — program name

e.g.

PURGE — SPHERV

This command may be used at any time to delete a program from the disk. It does not affect the program in the CPU.

Example

To illustrate this use of these commands, consider the following session at a terminal.

(Assume the connection with the computer has been made.)

(return) (line feed)	(This clears the line and verifies the connection)
<u>PLEASE LOG IN</u> HELLO — Z100, UVA	(The computer may cross out this line to keep your code number and password confidential)
<u>READY</u>	(The computer is ready for you to type a command or enter a program)
10 REM SAMPLE PROGRAM 40 PRINT "A = " A, "B = " B 20 READ A, B 30 DATA 1, 2 50 END	This short program is typed in. Note that the line numbers are not entered in sequential order.
LIST	The computer is instructed to print out the program currently in the CPU

```
10   REM SAMPLE PROGRAM
20   READ A, B
30   DATA 1, 2
40   PRINT "A = "; A, "B = "; B
50   END
```
{ The program is listed. Note that the line numbers are now in sequential order.

```
NAME – SAMP
```
{ The name SAMP is assigned to the program entered above

```
SAVE
```
{ The program named SAMP is saved on the disk. This does not affect the CPU. SAMP is still in the CPU.

```
SCRATCH
```
{ (The program SAMP is cleared from the CPU.)

```
10   PRINT "TEST"
20   END
```
{ A new program is entered.

```
LIST
```

```
10   PRINT "TEST"
20   END
```
{ The new program is listed.

```
GET–SAMP
```
{ The CPU memory is cleared and the program SAMP is copied into the CPU.

```
30   DATA 4,5
```
{ line 30 is modified

```
PURGE – SAMP
```
{ The unmodified (old) version of SAMP is removed from the disk.

```
SAVE
```
{ The new modified version is saved.

The Catalog

The computer maintains a list of the programs you have saved. This list, called the catalog, can be retrieved by typing

CATALOG (return)

It is useful to do this from time to time to be sure that you have deleted all programs which have outlived their usefulness.

VERSION B

Logging In

After establishing contact with the computer, the procedure for identifying yourself or logging in is straight forward.

The procedure begins by typing a carriage return. The computer will respond by asking you for your user number which is entered as shown

<u>USER NUMBER</u> — Z100 (return)

Since many time-sharing computers have more than one programming language available, you must indicate which one you wish to use. The computer will ask which system you want. The proper response is BASIC. For example

<u>SYSTEM</u> — BASIC (return)

Next, the computer will ask whether an old program is to be run or a new program is to be entered. If you wish to run an old program, the appropriate response is old. To enter a new program, respond with new.

The sequence may go as follows:

<u>OLD OR NEW</u> — OLD (return)
<u>OLD FILE NAME</u> — SAMPLE (return)

Here SAMPLE is the name of the old program you wish to recall to the CPU. The computer will now type <u>READY</u>. The program SAMPLE will now be in the CPU for you to run or modify. To see what is there, the LIST command must be used.

For a new program, the sequence is

<u>OLD OR NEW</u> — NEW (return)
<u>NEW FILE NAME</u> — TEST (return)

Test is the name now assigned to the program you are about to enter. The CPU is now clear and the computer will type

READY

You may type OLD or NEW at any time and the computer will respond with

OLD FILE NAME

or

NEW FILE NAME

and the sequence proceeds as above. These commands clear the CPU.

Saving a Program

Often it is convenient to save a program (on the disk) for future use. This is especially useful when developing long programs or when programs are used many times.

When the program is in the form which is to be saved, type

SAVE

After a program has been saved, you may continue to modify it. However, any changes made after the SAVE command are made only in the CPU — not on the disk.

Eliminating a Saved Program

If you wish to retain changes you made in a previously saved program, the old version must be eliminated from the disk before the revised version can be stored. This is accomplished by typing

UNSAVE — program name

e.g.

UNSAVE — SAMP

Now the revised version can be saved by using the SAVE command.

Another reason for eliminating saved programs is that there is usually limited disk space available. Thus, to make room for new programs, old programs which are no longer useful should be removed from the disk.

Example

The following sample session illustrates the use of these commands. (Assume the connection with the computer has been established.)

(return)	(This clears the line and verifies the connection.)
USER NUMBER – Z100	The user number is asked for and entered.
SYSTEM – BASIC	The programming language desired is BASIC.
OLD OR NEW – NEW	A new program is to be entered.
NEW FILE NAME – SAMP	The new program is called SAMP.
READY	The computer is now ready for you to enter SAMP.
10 REM SAMPLE PROGRAM 40 PRINT "A = "; A, "B = "; B 20 READ A, B 30 DATA 1, 2 50 END	SAMP is now entered. Note that the lines are not entered in numerical order.
LIST	The computer is instructed to print the program currently in the CPU.
10 REM SAMPLE PROGRAM 20 READ A, B 30 DATA 1, 2 40 PRINT "A = "; A, "B = "; B 50 END	The program is listed. Note that the lines are now arranged in numerical order.

SAVE $\left\{\begin{array}{l}\text{The program SAMP is saved on the}\\ \text{disk. The program remains unchanged}\\ \text{in the CPU.}\end{array}\right.$

NEW $\left\{\begin{array}{l}\text{This clears ("erases") SAMP from the}\\ \text{CPU and prepares the system for a}\\ \text{new program.}\end{array}\right.$

NEW FILE NAME — TEST $\left\{\begin{array}{l}\text{The new program is assigned the name}\\ \text{"test".}\end{array}\right.$

READY $\left\{\begin{array}{l}\text{The computer is now ready to accept}\\ \text{the new program, TEST.}\end{array}\right.$

10 PRINT "TEST"
20 END $\left\{\text{The program TEST is entered.}\right.$

LIST

10 PRINT "TEST"
20 END $\left\{\text{The program TEST is listed.}\right.$

OLD

OLD FILE NAME — SAMP $\left\{\begin{array}{l}\text{The CPU is cleared. SAMP is copied}\\ \text{to the CPU.}\end{array}\right.$

30 DATA 4, 5 $\left\{\text{line 30 is changed}\right.$

UNSAVE — SAMP $\left\{\text{The old version of SAMP is deleted.}\right.$

SAVE $\left\{\begin{array}{l}\text{The modified (line 30) version of}\\ \text{SAMP is saved.}\end{array}\right.$

The Catalog

The computer maintains a list of the programs you have saved. This list, called the catalog, can be retrieved by typing

CATALOG (return)

It is useful to do this from time to time to be sure that you have deleted all programs which have outlived their usefulness.

Index